Travel phrasebooks collection
«Everything Will Be Okay!»

CW00673069

PHRASEBOOK

- ARMENIAN -

THE MOST IMPORTANT PHRASES

This phrasebook contains the most important phrases and questions for basic communication Everything you need to survive overseas

By Andrey Taranov

T&P BOOKS

Phrasebook + 1500-word dictionary

English-Armenian phrasebook & concise dictionary

By Andrey Taranov

The collection of "Everything Will Be Okay" travel phrasebooks published by T&P Books is designed for people traveling abroad for tourism and business. The phrasebooks contain what matters most - the essentials for basic communication. This is an indispensable set of phrases to "survive" while abroad.

Another section of the book also provides a small dictionary with more than 1,500 useful words arranged alphabetically. The dictionary includes a lot of gastronomic terms and will be helpful when ordering food at a restaurant or buying groceries at the store.

T&P Books Publishing
www.tpbooks.com

ISBN: 978-1-78492-446-1

This book is also available in E-book formats.
Please visit www.tpbooks.com or the major online bookstores.

FOREWORD

The collection of "Everything Will Be Okay" travel phrasebooks published by T&P Books is designed for people traveling abroad for tourism and business. The phrasebooks contain what matters most - the essentials for basic communication. This is an indispensable set of phrases to "survive" while abroad.

This phrasebook will help you in most cases where you need to ask something, get directions, find out how much something costs, etc. It can also resolve difficult communication situations where gestures just won't help.

This book contains a lot of phrases that have been grouped according to the most relevant topics. A separate section of the book also provides a small dictionary with more than 1,500 important and useful words.

Take "Everything Will Be Okay" phrasebook with you on the road and you'll have an irreplaceable traveling companion who will help you find your way out of any situation and teach you to not fear speaking with foreigners.

TABLE OF CONTENTS

T&P Books Publishing

PRONUNCIATION

Letter	Armenian example	T&P phonetic alphabet	English example

Vowels

Letter	Armenian example	T&P phonetic alphabet	English example
ա	սաq	[ɑ]	shorter than in park, card
ե [1]	եյակ	[e]	elm, medal
ե [2]	մեխակ	[ɛ]	man, bad
է	էժան	[ɛ]	man, bad
ի	միս	[i]	shorter than in feet
ո [3]	ոգեի	[vɔ]	divorce, to avoid
ո [4]	բողոքել	[o]	pod, John
ու	թոշուն	[u]	book
օ [5]	օգտվել	[o]	pod, John
ը	ընտրել	[ə]	driver, teacher

Consonants

Letter	Armenian example	T&P phonetic alphabet	English example
բ	բարձր	[b]	baby, book
գ	գագաթ	[g]	game, gold
դ	դերանուն	[d]	day, doctor
զ	զվարճանալ	[z]	zebra, please
թ	թև	[th]	don't have
ժ	ժամացույց	[ʒ]	forge, pleasure
լ	լլացվել	[l]	lace, people
խ	ախտորոշում	[h], [x]	as in Scots loch
ծ	ծիածան	[ts]	cats, tsetse fly
կ	փակել	[k]	clock, kiss
հ	նիհարել	[h]	home, have
ձ	ձանրածող	[dz]	beads, kids
ղ	մերք	[ɣ]	between [g] and [h]
ճ	ճահիճ	[tʃ]	church, French
մ	ամայի	[m]	magic, milk
յ	նայել	[j]	yes, New York
ն	կանգառ	[n]	name, normal
շ	շուն	[ʃ]	machine, shark
չ	կրակայրիչ	[tʃh]	hitchhiker
պ	ամպ	[p]	pencil, private

Letter	Armenian example	T&P phonetic alphabet	English example
Ջ	գիշեր	[dʒ]	joke, general
ռ	տառ	[r]	rice, radio
ս	մաս	[s]	city, boss
վ	ավել	[v]	very, river
տ	պատուհան	[t]	tourist, trip
ր	կարել	[r]	soft [r]
ց	բաց	[tsh]	let's handle it
փ	սարսափ	[ph]	top hat
ք	դեմք	[k]	clock, kiss
ֆ	ասֆալտ	[f]	face, food

Comments

[1] at the beginning of a word
[2] in the middle
[3] at the beginning of a word
[4] in the middle
[5] at the beginning of a word usually

LIST OF ABBREVIATIONS

English abbreviations

ab.	-	about
adj	-	adjective
adv	-	adverb
anim.	-	animate
as adj	-	attributive noun used as adjective
e.g.	-	for example
etc.	-	et cetera
fam.	-	familiar
fem.	-	feminine
form.	-	formal
inanim.	-	inanimate
masc.	-	masculine
math	-	mathematics
mil.	-	military
n	-	noun
pl	-	plural
pron.	-	pronoun
sb	-	somebody
sing.	-	singular
sth	-	something
v aux	-	auxiliary verb
vi	-	intransitive verb
vi, vt	-	intransitive, transitive verb
vt	-	transitive verb

Armenian punctuation

՛	-	Exclamation mark
՞	-	Question mark
,	-	Comma

ARMENIAN
PHRASEBOOK

This section contains
important phrases that may
come in handy in various
real-life situations.
The phrasebook will help
you ask for directions, clarify
a price, buy tickets, and
order food at a restaurant

T&P Books Publishing

PHRASEBOOK CONTENTS

T&P Books Publishing

The bare minimum

Excuse me, ...
Ներեցեք, ...
[nerets'eq, ...]

Hello.
Բարև Ձեզ:
[bar'ev dzez]

Thank you.
Շնորհակալություն:
[shnorhakaluty'un]

Good bye.
Ցտեսություն:
[tstesuty'un]

Yes.
Այո:
[ay'o]

No.
Ոչ:
[voch]

I don't know.
Ես չգիտեմ:
[yes chgit'em]

Where? | Where to? | When?
Ո՞րտեղ: Ո՞ւր: Ե՞րբ:
[vort'egh? ur? yerb?]

I need ...
Ինձ հարկավոր է ...
[indz harkav'or e ...]

I want ...
Ես ուզում եմ ...
[yes uz'um em ...]

Do you have ...?
Դուք ունե՞ք ...:
[duq un'eq ...?]

Is there a ... here?
Այստեղ կա՞ ...:
[ayst'egh ka ...?]

May I ...?
Ես կարո՞ղ եմ ...:
[yes kar'ogh em ...?]

..., please (polite request)
Խնդրում եմ
[khndrum em]

I'm looking for ...
Ես փնտրում եմ ...
[yes pntrum am ...]

restroom
զուգարան
[zugar'an]

ATM
բանկոմատ
[bankom'at]

pharmacy (drugstore)
դեղատուն
[deghat'un]

hospital
հիվանդանոց
[hivandan'ots]

police station
ոստիկանության բաժանմունք
[vostikanuty'an bazhanm'unq]

subway
մետրո
[metr'o]

taxi	տաքսի [tax'i]
train station	կայարան [kayar'an]

My name is ...	Իմ անունը ... է: [im an'uny ... e]
What's your name?	Ձեր անունն ի՞նչ է: [dzer an'unn inch e?]
Could you please help me?	Օգնեցեք ինձ, խնդրեմ: [ognets'eq indz, khndrem]
I've got a problem.	Ես խնդիր ունեմ: [yes khndir un'em]
I don't feel well.	Ես ինձ վատ եմ զգում: [yes indz vat am zgum]
Call an ambulance!	Շտապ օգնություն կանչեք: [shtap ognuty'un kanch'eq!]
May I make a call?	Կարո՞ղ եմ զանգահարել: [kar'ogh am zangahar'el?]

I'm sorry.	Ներեցեք [nerets'eq]
You're welcome.	Խնդրեմ [kndrem]

I, me	Ես [yes]
you (inform.)	դու [du]
he	նա [na]
she	նա [na]
they (masc.)	նրանք [nrank]
they (fem.)	նրանք [nrank]
we	մենք [menq]
you (pl)	դուք [duq]
you (sg, form.)	Դուք [duq]

ENTRANCE	ՄՈՒՏՔ [mutq]
EXIT	ԵԼՔ [yelq]
OUT OF ORDER	ՉԻ ԱՇԽԱՏՈՒՄ [chi ashkhat'um]
CLOSED	ՓԱԿ Է [pak e]

OPEN	ԲԱՑ Է
	[bats e]
FOR WOMEN	ԿԱՆԱՆՑ ՀԱՄԱՐ
	[kan'ants ham'ar]
FOR MEN	ՏՂԱՄԱՐԴԿԱՆՑ ՀԱՄԱՐ
	[tghamardk'ants ham'ar]

Questions

Where?	Որտե՞ղ: [vort'egh?]
Where to?	Ո՞ւր: [ur?]
Where from?	Որտեղի՞ց: [vortegh'its?]
Why?	Ինչո՞ւ: [inch'u?]
For what reason?	Ինչի՞ համար: [inch'i ham'ar?]
When?	Ե՞րբ: [yerb?]
How long?	Ինչքա՞ն ժամանակ: [inchq'an zhaman'ak?]
At what time?	Ժամը քանիսի՞ն: [zh'amy qanis'in?]
How much?	Ի՞նչ արժե: [inch arzh'e?]
Do you have ...?	Դուք ունե՞ք ...: [duq un'eq ...?]
Where is ...?	Որտե՞ղ է գտնվում ...: [vort'egh e gtnvum ...?]
What time is it?	Ժամը քանի՞սն է: [zh'amy qan'isn e?]
May I make a call?	Կարո՞ղ եմ զանգահարել: [kar'ogh am zangahar'el?]
Who's there?	Ո՞վ է: [ov e?]
Can I smoke here?	Կարո՞ղ եմ այստեղ ծխել: [kar'ogh am ayst'egh tskhel?]
May I ...?	Ես կարո՞ղ եմ ...: [yes kar'ogh em ...?]

Needs

I'd like …	Ես կուզենայի … [yes kuzen'ayi …]
I don't want …	Ես չեմ ուզում … [yes chem uz'um …]
I'm thirsty.	Ես ծարավ եմ: [yes tsar'av am]
I want to sleep.	Ես ուզում եմ քնել: [yes uz'um am qnel]
I want …	Ես ուզում եմ … [yes uz'um am …]
to wash up	լվացվել [lvatsv'el]
to brush my teeth	ատամներս մաքրել [atamn'ers maqr'el]
to rest a while	մի քիչ հանգստանալ [mi qich hangstan'al]
to change my clothes	շորերս փոխել [shor'ers pokh'el]
to go back to the hotel	վերադառնալ հյուրանոց [veradarn'al hyuran'ots]
to buy …	գնել … [gnel …]
to go to …	գնալ … [gnal …]
to visit …	այցելել … [aytsel'el …]
to meet with …	հանդիպել … հետ [handip'el … het]
to make a call	զանգահարել [zangahar'el]
I'm tired.	Ես հոգնել եմ: [yes hogn'el am]
We are tired.	Մենք հոգնել ենք: [menq hogn'el enq]
I'm cold.	Ես մրսում եմ: [yes mrsum am]
I'm hot.	Ես շոգում եմ: [yes shog'um am]
I'm OK.	Ես լավ եմ: [yes lav am]

I need to make a call.

Ես պետք է զանգահարեմ:
[yes petq e zangahar'em]

I need to go to the restroom.

Ես զուգարան եմ ուզում:
[yes zugar'an am uz'um]

I have to go.

Գնալու ժամանակն է:
[gnal'us zhaman'akn e]

I have to go now.

Ես պետք է գնամ:
[yes petq e gnam]

Asking for directions

Excuse me, ...	Ներեցեք, ... [nerets'eq, ...]
Where is ...?	Որտե՞ղ է գտնվում ... [vort'egh e gtnvum ...?]
Which way is ...?	Ո՞ր ուղղությամբ է գտնվում ... [vor ughghuty'amb e gtnv'um ...?]
Could you help me, please?	Օգնեցեք ինձ, խնդրեմ: [ognets'eq indz, khndrem]
I'm looking for ...	Ես փնտրում եմ ... [yes pntrum am ...]
I'm looking for the exit.	Ես փնտրում եմ ելքը: [yes pntrum am y'elky]
I'm going to ...	Ես գնում եմ ... [yes gnum am ...]
Am I going the right way to ...?	Ես ճի՞շտ եմ գնում ...: [yes chisht am gnum ...?]
Is it far?	Դա հեռո՞ւ է: [da her'u e?]
Can I get there on foot?	Ես կհասնե՞մ այնտեղ ոտքով: [yes khasn'em aynt'egh votq'ov?]
Can you show me on the map?	Ցույց տվեք ինձ քարտեզի վրա, խնդրում եմ: [tsuyts tveq indz qartez'i vra, khndrum am]
Show me where we are right now.	Ցույց տվեք` որտեղ ենք մենք հիմա: [tsuyts tveq vort'egh enk menq him'a]
Here	Այստեղ [ayst'egh]
There	Այնտեղ [aynt'egh]
This way	Այստեղ [ayst'egh]
Turn right.	Թեքվեք աջ: [tekv'ek aj]
Turn left.	Թեքվեք ձախ: [tekv'ek dzakh]
first (second, third) turn	առաջին (երկրորդ, երրորդ) շրջադարձ [araj'in (yerkr'ord, err'ord) shrjad'ardz]
to the right	դեպի աջ [dep'i aj]

to the left

դեպի ձախ
[dep'i dzakh]

Go straight.

Գնացեք ուղիղ:
[gnats'ek ugh'igh]

Signs

WELCOME!	ԲԱՐԻ~ ԳԱԼՈՒՍՏ: [bar'i gal'ust!]
ENTRANCE	ՄՈՒՏՔ [mutq]
EXIT	ԵԼՔ [yelq]

PUSH	ԴԵՊԻ ՆԵՐՍ [dep'i ners]
PULL	ԴԵՊԻ ԴՈՒՐՍ [dep'i durs]
OPEN	ԲԱՑ Է [bats e]
CLOSED	ՓԱԿ Է [pak e]

FOR WOMEN	ԿԱՆԱՆՑ ՀԱՄԱՐ [kan'ants ham'ar]
FOR MEN	ՏՂԱՄԱՐԴԿԱՆՑ ՀԱՄԱՐ [tghamardk'ants ham'ar]
MEN, GENTS	ՏՂԱՄԱՐԴԿԱՆՑ ԶՈՒԳԱՐԱՆ [tghamardk'ants zugar'an]
WOMEN, LADIES	ԿԱՆԱՆՑ ԶՈՒԳԱՐԱՆ [kan'ants zugar'an]

DISCOUNTS	ԶԵՂՉ [zeghch]
SALE	ԻՍՊԱՌ ՎԱՃԱՌՔ [isp'ar vach'ark]
FREE	ԱՆՎՃԱՐ [anvch'ar]
NEW!	ՆՈՐՈ՛ՒՅԹ [nor'uyt]
ATTENTION!	ՈՒՇԱԴՐՈՒԹՅՈ՛ՒՆ [ushadruty'un]

NO VACANCIES	ԱԶԱՏ ՀԱՄԱՐՆԵՐ ՉԿԱՆ [az'at hamarn'er chk'an]
RESERVED	ՊԱՏՎԻՐՎԱԾ Է [patvirv'ats e]
ADMINISTRATION	ԱԴՄԻՆԻՍՏՐԱՑԻԱ [administratsi'a]
STAFF ONLY	ՄԻԱՅՆ ԱՆՁՆԱԿԱԶՄԻ ՀԱՄԱՐ [mi'ayn andznakazm'i ham'ar]

BEWARE OF THE DOG!	ԿԱՍՏԱՂԱԾ ՇՈՒՆ [katagh'ats shun]
NO SMOKING!	ՉԾԽԵ՛Լ [chtskh'el]
DO NOT TOUCH!	ՁԵՌՔԵՐՈՎ ՉԴԻՊՉԵԼ [dzerkyer'ov chdipch'el]
DANGEROUS	ՎՏԱՆԳԱՎՈՐ Է [vtangav'or e]
DANGER	ՎՏԱՆԳ [vtang]
HIGH VOLTAGE	ԲԱՐՁՐ ԼԱՐՈՒՄ [bardzr lar'um]
NO SWIMMING!	ԼՈՂԱԼՆ ԱՐԳԵԼՎՈՒՄ Է [logh'aln argelv'um e]
OUT OF ORDER	ՉԻ ԱՇԽԱՏՈՒՄ [chi ashkhat'um]
FLAMMABLE	ԴՅՈՒՐԱՎԱՌ Է [dyurav'ar e]
FORBIDDEN	ԱՐԳԵԼՎԱԾ Է [argelv'ats e]
NO TRESPASSING!	ՄՈՒՏՔՆ ԱՐԳԵԼՎԱԾ Է [mutkn argelv'ats e]
WET PAINT	ՆԵՐԿՎԱԾ Է [nerkv'ats e]
CLOSED FOR RENOVATIONS	ՓԱԿՎԱԾ Է ՎԵՐԱՆՈՐՈԳՄԱՆ [pakv'ats e veranorogm'an]
WORKS AHEAD	ՎԵՐԱՆՈՐՈԳՄԱՆ ԱՇԽԱՏԱՆՔՆԵՐ [veranorogm'an ashkhatankn'er]
DETOUR	ՇՐՋԱՆՑՈՒՄ [shrjants'um]

Transportation. General phrases

plane	ինքնաթիռ [inqnat'ir]
train	գնացք [gnatsq]
bus	ավտոբուս [avtob'us]
ferry	լաստանավ [lastanav]
taxi	տաքսի [tax'i]
car	ավտոմեքենա [avtomeqen'a]
schedule	չվացուցակ [chvatsuts'ak]
Where can I see the schedule?	Որտե՞ղ կարելի է նայել չվացուցակը: [vort'egh karel'i e nay'el chvatsuts'aky?]
workdays (weekdays)	աշխատանքային օրեր [ashkhatankay'in or'er]
weekends	հանգստյան օրեր [hangsty'an or'er]
holidays	տոնական օրեր [tonak'an or'er]
DEPARTURE	ՄԵԿՆՈՒՄ [mekn'um]
ARRIVAL	ԺԱՄԱՆՈՒՄ [zhaman'um]
DELAYED	ՈՒՇԱՑՈՒՄ [ushats'um]
CANCELED	ՉԵՂՅԱԼ [cheghy'al]
next (train, etc.)	հաջորդ [haj'ord]
first	առաջին [araj'in]
last	վերջին [verj'in]
When is the next ...?	Ե՞րբ է լինելու հաջորդ ...: [yerb e linel'u haj'ordy ...?]
When is the first ...?	Ե՞րբ է մեկնում առաջին ...: [yerb e mekn'um araj'in ...?]

When is the last ...?

Ե՞րբ է մեկնում վերջին ...:
[yerb e mekn'um verj'in ...?]

transfer (change of trains, etc.)

նստափոխ
[nstap'okh]

to make a transfer

նստափոխ կատարել
[nstap'okh katar'el]

Do I need to make a transfer?

Ես պետք է նստափոՙխ կատարեմ:
[yes petq e nstap'okh katar'em?]

Buying tickets

Where can I buy tickets?	Որտե՞ղ կարող եմ տոմսեր գնել: [vort'egh kar'ogh am toms'er gnel?]
ticket	տոմս [toms]
to buy a ticket	տոմս գնել [toms gnel]
ticket price	տոմսի արժեքը [t'omsi arzh'eqy]
Where to?	Ո՞ւր: [ur?]
To what station?	Մինչև ո՞ր կայարան: [minch'ev vor kayar'an?]
I need ...	Ինձ հարկավոր է ... [indz harkav'or e ...]
one ticket	մեկ տոմս [mek toms]
two tickets	երկու տոմս [yerk'u toms]
three tickets	երեք տոմս [yer'ek toms]
one-way	մեկ ուղղությամբ [mek ughghuty'amb]
round-trip	վերադարձով [veradardz'ov]
first class	առաջին դաս [araj'in das]
second class	երկրորդ դաս [yerkr'ord das]
today	այսոր [ays'or]
tomorrow	վաղը [v'aghy]
the day after tomorrow	վաղը չէ մյուս օրը [v'aghy che my'us 'ory]
in the morning	առավոտյան [aravoty'an]
in the afternoon	ցերեկը [tser'eky]
in the evening	երեկոյան [yerekoy'an]

aisle seat

տեղ միջանցքի մոտ
[tegh mijantsk'i mot]

window seat

տեղ պատուհանի մոտ
[tegh patuhan'i mot]

How much?

Ինչքա՞ն:
[inchq'an?]

Can I pay by credit card?

Կարո՞ղ եմ վճարել քարտով:
[kar'ogh am vchar'el qart'ov?]

Bus

bus	ավտոբուս [avtob'us]
intercity bus	միջքաղաքային ավտոբուս [mijqaghaqay'in avtob'us]
bus stop	ավտոբուսի կանգառ [avtob'usi kang'ar]
Where's the nearest bus stop?	Որտե՞ղ է մոտակա ավտոբուսի կանգառը: [vort'egh e motak'a avtob'usi kang'ary?]

number (bus ~, etc.)	համար [ham'ar]
Which bus do I take to get to ...?	Ո՞ր ավտոբուսն է գնում մինչև ...: [vor avtob'usn e gnum minch'ev ...?]
Does this bus go to ...?	Այս ավտոբուսը գնո՞ւմ է մինչև ...: [ays avtob'usy gnum e minch'ev ...?]
How frequent are the buses?	Որքա՞ն հաճախ են գնում ավտոբուսները: [vorq'an hach'akh en gnum avtob'usnery?]

every 15 minutes	յուրաքանչյուր տասնհինգ րոպեն մեկ [yurakanchy'ur tasnh'ing rop'en mek]
every half hour	յուրաքանչյուր կեսժամը մեկ [yurakanchy'ur kes jam'y mek]
every hour	յուրաքանչյուր ժամը մեկ [yurakanchy'ur jam'y mek]
several times a day	օրեկան մի քանի անգամ [orek'an mi qan'i ang'am]
... times a day	օրեկան ... անգամ [orek'an ... ang'am]

schedule	չվացուցակ [chvatsuts'ak]
Where can I see the schedule?	Որտե՞ղ կարելի է նայել չվացուցակը: [vort'egh kareli e nay'el chvatsuts'aky?]
When is the next bus?	Ե՞րբ է լինելու հաջորդ ավտոբուսը: [yerb e linel'u haj'ord avtob'usy?]
When is the first bus?	Ե՞րբ է մեկնում առաջին ավտոբուսը: [yerb e mekn'um araj'in avtob'usy?]
When is the last bus?	Ե՞րբ է մեկնում վերջին ավտոբուսը: [yerb e mekn'um verj'in avtob'usy?]

stop

next stop

last stop (terminus)

Stop here, please.

Excuse me, this is my stop.

կանգառ
[kang'ar]

հաջորդ կանգառ
[haj'ord kang'ar]

վերջին կանգառ
[verj'in kang'ar]

Կանգնեք այստեղ, խնդրում եմ:
[kangn'ek ayst'egh, khndrum em]

Թույլ տվեք, սա իմ կանգառն է:
[tuyl tveq, sa im kang'arn e]

Train

train	գնացք [gnatsq]
suburban train	մերձքաղաքային գնացք [merdzqaghaqay'in gnatsq]
long-distance train	հեռագնաց գնացք [heragn'ac gnatsq]
train station	կայարան [kayar'an]
Excuse me, where is the exit to the platform?	Ներեցեք, որտե՞ղ է ելքը դեպի գնացքները: [nerets'eq, vort'egh e y'elky dep'i gnatsqn'ery?]

Does this train go to ...?	Այս գնացքը գնու՞մ է մինչև ...: [ays gn'atsqy gnum e minch'ev ...?]
next train	հաջորդ գնացքը [haj'ord gn'atsqy]
When is the next train?	Ե՞րբ է լինելու հաջորդ գնացքը: [yerb e linel'u haj'ord gn'atsqy?]
Where can I see the schedule?	Որտե՞ղ կարելի է նայել չվացուցակը: [vort'egh karel'i e nay'el chvatsuts'aky?]
From which platform?	Ո՞ր հարթակից: [vor hartak'its?]
When does the train arrive in ...?	Ե՞րբ է գնացքը ժամանում ...: [yerb e gn'atsqy zhaman'um ...?]

Please help me.	Օգնեցեք ինձ, խնդրեմ: [ognets'eq indz, khndrem]
I'm looking for my seat.	Ես փնտրում եմ իմ տեղը: [yes pntrum am im t'eghy]
We're looking for our seats.	Մենք փնտրում ենք մեր տեղերը: [menq pntrum enq mer tegh'ery]

My seat is taken.	Իմ տեղը զբաղված է: [im t'eghy zbaghv'ats e]
Our seats are taken.	Մեր տեղերը զբաղված են: [mer tegh'ery zbaghv'ats en]
I'm sorry but this is my seat.	Ներեցեք, խնդրում եմ, բայց սա իմ տեղն է: [nerets'eq, khndrum am, bayts sa im t'eghn e]

Is this seat taken?

Uյս տեղն ազա՞տ է:
[ays teghn az'at e?]

May I sit here?

Կարո՞ղ եմ այստեղ նստել:
[kar'ogh am ayst'egh nstel?]

On the train. Dialogue (No ticket)

Ticket, please.

Չեր տոմսը, խնդրեմ:
[dzer t'omsy, khndrem]

I don't have a ticket.

Ես տոմս չունեմ:
[yes toms chun'em]

I lost my ticket.

Ես կորցրել եմ իմ տոմսը:
[yes kortsr'el am im t'omsy]

I forgot my ticket at home.

Ես մոռացել եմ իմ տոմսը տանը:
[yes morats'el am im t'omsy t'any]

You can buy a ticket from me.

Դուք կարող եք գնել տոմս ինձանից:
[indzan'its]

You will also have to pay a fine.

Նաև դուք պետք է վճարեք տուգանք:
[na'ev duq petq e vchar'eq tug'ank]

Okay.

Լավ:
[lav]

Where are you going?

Ո՞ւր եք մեկնում:
[ur eq mekn'um?]

I'm going to …

Ես գնում եմ մինչև …
[yes gnum am minch'ev …]

How much? I don't understand.

Ինչքա՞ն է: Ես չեմ հասկանում:
[inchq'an? yes chem haskan'um]

Write it down, please.

Գրեք, խնդրում եմ:
[grek, khndrum em]

Okay. Can I pay with a credit card?

Լավ: Կարո՞ղ եմ վճարել քարտով:
[lav kar'ogh am vchar'el qart'ov?]

Yes, you can.

Այո, կարող եք:
[ay'o, kar'ogh eq]

Here's your receipt.

Ահա ձեր անդորրագիրը:
[ah'a dzer andorag'iry]

Sorry about the fine.

Ցավում եմ տուգանքի համար:
[tsav'um am tugank'i ham'ar]

That's okay. It was my fault.

Ոչինչ: Դա իմ մեղքն է:
[voch'inch. da im meghqn e]

Enjoy your trip.

Հաճելի ճանապարհորդությու՛ն:
[hachel'i chanaparhoduty'un]

Taxi

taxi	տաքսի [tax'i]
taxi driver	տաքսու վարորդ [tax'u var'ord]
to catch a taxi	տաքսի բռնել [tax'i brnel]
taxi stand	տաքսու կանգառ [tax'u kang'ar]
Where can I get a taxi?	Որտե՞ղ կարող եմ տաքսի վերցնել: [vort'egh kar'ogh am tax'i vertsn'el?]
to call a taxi	տաքսի կանչել [tax'i kanch'el]
I need a taxi.	Ինձ տաքսի է հարկավոր: [indz tax'i e harkav'or]
Right now.	Հենց հիմա: [hents him'a]
What is your address (location)?	Ձեր հասցե՞ն: [dzer hasc'en?]
My address is ...	Իմ հասցեն ... [im hasc'en ...]
Your destination?	Ո՞ւր եք գնալու: [ur eq gnal'u?]
Excuse me, ...	Ներեցեք, ... [nerets'eq, ...]
Are you available?	Ազա՞տ եք: [az'at eq?]
How much is it to get to ...?	Ի՞նչ արժե հասնել մինչև ...: [inch arzh'e hasn'el minch'ev ...?]
Do you know where it is?	Դուք գիտե՞ք՝ որտեղ է դա: [duq git'eq vort'egh e da?]
Airport, please.	Օդանավակայան, խնդրում եմ: [odanavakay'an, khndrum em]
Stop here, please.	Կանգնեցրեք այստեղ, խնդրում եմ: [kangnetsr'eq ayst'egh, khndrum em]
It's not here.	Դա այստեղ չէ: [da ayst'egh che]
This is the wrong address.	Դա սխալ հասցե է: [da skhal hasc'e e]
Turn left.	դեպի ձախ [dep'i dzakh]
Turn right.	դեպի աջ [dep'i aj]

How much do I owe you?	Որքա՞ն պետք է վճարեմ:
	[vorq'an petq e vchar'em?]
I'd like a receipt, please.	Տվեք ինձ չեքը, խնդրում եմ:
	[tveq indz ch'eqy, khndrum em]
Keep the change.	Մանրը պետք չէ:
	[m'anry petq che]

Would you please wait for me?	Սպասեք ինձ, խնդրում եմ:
	[spas'eq indz, khndrum em]
five minutes	հինգ րոպե
	[hing rop'e]
ten minutes	տաս րոպե
	[tas rop'e]
fifteen minutes	տասնհինգ րոպե
	[tasnh'ing rop'e]
twenty minutes	քսան րոպե
	[qsan rop'e]
half an hour	կես ժամ
	[kes zham]

Hotel

Hello.
Բարև Ձեզ:
[bar'ev dzez]

My name is ...
Իմ անունը ... է:
[im an'uny ... e]

I have a reservation.
Ես համար եմ ամրագրել:
[yes ham'ar am amragr'el]

I need ...
Ինձ հարկավոր է ...
[indz harkav'or e ...]

a single room
մեկտեղանոց համար
[mekteghan'ots ham'ar]

a double room
երկտեղանոց համար
[yerkteghan'ots ham'ar]

How much is that?
Որքա՞ն այն արժե:
[vorq'an ayn arzh'e?]

That's a bit expensive.
Դա մի քիչ թանկ է:
[da mi qich tank'e]

Do you have any other options?
Ունե՞ք որևէ այլ տարբերակ:
[un'eq vorev'e 'ayl tarber'ak?]

I'll take it.
Ես դա կվերցնեմ:
[yes da kvertsn'em]

I'll pay in cash.
Ես կանխիկ կվճարեմ:
[yes kankh'ik kvchar'em]

I've got a problem.
Ես խնդիր ունեմ:
[yes khnd'ir un'em]

My ... is broken.
Իմ ... փչացել է:
[im ... pchats'el e]

My ... is out of order.
Իմ ... չի աշխատում:
[im ... chi ashkhat'um]

TV
հեռուստացույցը
[herustats'uytsy]

air conditioning
օդորակիչը
[odorak'ichy]

tap
ծորակը
[tsor'aky]

shower
ցնցուղը
[tsnts'ughy]

sink
լվացարանը
[lvatsar'any]

safe
չհրկիզվող պահարանը
[chhrkizv'ogh pahar'any]

door lock	կողպեքը [koghp'eqy]
electrical outlet	վարդակը [vard'aky]
hairdryer	ֆենը [f'eny]
I don't have ...	Ես ... չունեմ: [yes ... chun'em]
water	ջուր [jur]
light	լույս [luys]
electricity	հոսանք [hos'anq]
Can you give me ...?	Կարո՞ղ եք ինձ տալ ...: [kar'ogh eq indz tal ...?]
a towel	սրբիչ [srbich]
a blanket	ծածկոց [tsatsk'ots]
slippers	հողաթափեր [hoghatap'er]
a robe	խալաթ [khal'at]
shampoo	շամպուն [shamp'un]
soap	օճառ [och'ar]
I'd like to change rooms.	Ես կցանկանայի փոխել համարս: [yes ktsankan'ayi pokh'el ham'ars]
I can't find my key.	Ես չեմ կարողանում գտնել իմ բանալին: [yes chem karoghan'um gtnel im banal'in]
Could you open my room, please?	Խնդրում եմ, բացեք իմ համարը: [khndrum em, bats'ek im ham'ary]
Who's there?	Ո՞վ է: [ov e?]
Come in!	Մտեք: [mteq!]
Just a minute!	Մեկ րոպե! [mek'rope!]
Not right now, please.	Խնդրում եմ, հիմա չէ: [khndrum em, him'a che]
Come to my room, please.	Խնդրում եմ, ինձ մոտ մտեք: [khndrum em, indz mot mteq]
I'd like to order food service.	Ես ուզում եմ ուտելիք համար պատվիրել: [yes uz'um am utel'iq ham'ar patvir'el]

My room number is …

Իմ սենյակի համարը … է:
[im senyak'i ham'ary … e]

I'm leaving …

Ես մեկնում եմ …
[yes mekn'um am …]

We're leaving …

Մենք մեկնում ենք …
[menq mekn'um enq …]

right now

հիմա
[him'a]

this afternoon

այսոր ճաշից հետո
[ays'or chash'its het'o]

tonight

այսոր երեկոյան
[ays'or yerekoy'an]

tomorrow

վաղը
[v'aghy]

tomorrow morning

վաղն առավոտյան
[v'aghn aravoty'an]

tomorrow evening

վաղը երեկոյան
[v'aghy yerekoy'an]

the day after tomorrow

վաղը չէ մյուս օրը
[v'aghy che my'us 'ory]

I'd like to pay.

Ես կուզենայի հաշիվը փակել:
[yes kuzen'ayi hash'ivy pak'el]

Everything was wonderful.

Ամեն ինչ հոյակապ էր:
[am'en inch hoyak'ap er]

Where can I get a taxi?

Որտե՞ղ կարող եմ տաքսի վերցնել:
[vort'egh kar'ogh am tax'i vertsn'el?]

Would you call a taxi for me, please?

Ինձ համար տաքսի կանչեք,
խնդրում եմ:
[indz ham'ar tax'i kanch'eq,
khndrum em]

Restaurant

Can I look at the menu, please?
Կարո՞ղ եմ նայել ձեր ճաշացանկը:
[kar'ogh am nay'el dzer chashats'anky?]

Table for one.
Սեղան մեկ հոգու համար:
[segh'an mek hog'u ham'ar]

There are two (three, four) of us.
Մենք երկուսով (երեքով, չորսով) ենք:
[menq yerkus'ov (yerek'ov, chors'ov) enq]

Smoking
Ծխողների համար
[tskhoghner'i ham'ar]

No smoking
Չծխողների համար
[chtskhoghner'i ham'ar]

Excuse me! (addressing a waiter)
Մոտեցեք խնդրեմ:
[motets'eq khndrem!]

menu
Ճաշացանկ
[chashats'ank]

wine list
Գինեքարտ
[gineq'art]

The menu, please.
Ճաշացանկը, խնդրեմ:
[chashats'anky, khndrem]

Are you ready to order?
Պատրա՞ստ եք պատվիրել:
[patr'ast eq patvir'el?]

What will you have?
Ի՞նչ եք պատվիրելու:
[inch eq patvirel'u?]

I'll have ...
Ես կվերցնեմ ...
[yes kvertsn'em ...]

I'm a vegetarian.
Ես բուսակեր եմ:
[yes busak'er am]

meat
միս
[mis]

fish
ձուկ
[dzuk]

vegetables
բանջարեղեն
[banjaregh'en]

Do you have vegetarian dishes?
Դուք ունե՞ք բուսակերական
ճաշատեսակներ:
[duq un'eq busakerak'an
chashatesakn'er?]

I don't eat pork.
Ես խոզի միս չեմ ուտում:
[yes kh'ozi mis chem ut'um]

He /she/ doesn't eat meat.
Նա միս չի ուտում:
[na mis chi ut'um]

I am allergic to ...

Ես ...ից ալերգիա ունեմ:
[yes ...its alerg'ia un'em]

Would you please bring me ...

Խնդրում եմ, ինձ ... բերեք:
[khndrum em, indz ... ber'eq]

salt | pepper | sugar

աղ | պղպեղ | շաքար
[agh | pghpegh | shaq'ar]

coffee | tea | dessert

սուրճ | թեյ | աղանդեր
[surch | tey | aghand'er]

water | sparkling | plain

ջուր | գազավորված | չգազավորված
[jur | gazavorv'ats | chgazavorv'ats]

a spoon | fork | knife

գդալ | պատառաքաղ | դանակ
[gdal | pataraq'agh | dan'ak]

a plate | napkin

ափսե | անձեռոցիկ
[aps'e | andzerots'ik]

Enjoy your meal!

Բարի ախորժա՛կ:
[bar'i akhorzh'ak!]

One more, please.

Էլի բերեք, խնդրում եմ:
[el'i ber'eq, khndrum em]

It was very delicious.

Շատ համեղ էր:
[shat ham'egh er]

check | change | tip

հաշիվ | մանրադրամ | թեյավճար
[hash'iv | manradr'am | tyeyavch'ar]

Check, please.
(Could I have the check, please?)

Հաշիվը, խնդրում եմ:
[hash'ivy, khndrum em]

Can I pay by credit card?

Կարո՞ղ եմ վճարել քարտով:
[kar'ogh am vchar'el qart'ov?]

I'm sorry, there's a mistake here.

Ներեցեք, այստեղ սխալ կա:
[nerets'eq, ayst'egh skhal ka]

Shopping

Can I help you?
Կարո՞ղ եմ օգնել ձեզ:
[kar'ogh am ogn'el dzez?]

Do you have ...?
Դուք ունե՞բ ...:
[duq un'eq ...?]

I'm looking for ...
Ես փնտրում եմ ...
[yes pntrum am ...]

I need ...
Ինձ պետք է ...
[indz petq e ...]

I'm just looking.
Ես ուղղակի նայում եմ:
[yes ughghak'i nay'um am]

We're just looking.
Մենք ուղղակի նայում ենք:
[menq ughgh'aki nay'um enq]

I'll come back later.
Ես ավելի ուշ կայցելեմ:
[yes avel'i ush kaytsel'em]

We'll come back later.
Մենք ավելի ուշ կայցելենք:
[menq avel'i ush kaytsel'enq]

discounts | sale
զեղչեր | իսպառ վաճառք
[zeghch'er | isp'ar vach'arq]

Would you please show me ...
Ցույց տվեք ինձ, խնդրում եմ ...
[tsuyts tveq indz, khndrum em ...]

Would you please give me ...
Տվեք ինձ, խնդրում եմ ...
[tveq indz, khndrum em ...]

Can I try it on?
Կարո՞ղ եմ ես սա փորձել:
[kar'ogh am yes sa pordz'el?]

Excuse me, where's the fitting room?
Ներեցեք, որտե՞ղ է հանդերձարանը:
[nerets'eq, vort'egh e handerdzar'any?]

Which color would you like?
Ի՞նչ գույն եք ուզում:
[inch guyn eq uz'um?]

size | length
չափս | հասակ
[chaps | hasak]

How does it fit?
Եղա՞վ:
[yegh'av?]

How much is it?
Սա ինչքա՞ն արժե:
[sa inchq'an arzh'e?]

That's too expensive.
Դա չափազանց թանկ է:
[da chapaz'ants tank e]

I'll take it.
Ես կվերցնեմ սա:
[yes kvertsn'em sa]

Excuse me, where do I pay?
Ներեցեք, որտե՞ղ է դրամարկղը:
[nerets'eq, vort'egh e dram'arkghy?]

Will you pay in cash or credit card?

Ինչպե՞ս եք վճարելու:
Կանխիկ կ թե քարտով:
[inchp'es eq vcharel'u?
kankh'ik te qart'ov?]

In cash | with credit card

կանխիկ | քարտով
[kankh'ik | qart'ov]

Do you want the receipt?

Ձեզ չեքն անհրաժե՞շտ է:
[dzez cheqn anhrazh'esht e?]

Yes, please.

Այո, խնդրում եմ:
[ay'o, khndrum em]

No, it's OK.

Ոչ, պետք չէ: Շնորհակալություն:
[voch, petq che. shnorhakaluty'un]

Thank you. Have a nice day!

Շնորհակալություն: Ցտեսություն:
[shnorhakaluty'un tstesuty'un!]

In town

Excuse me, please.	Ներեցեք խնդրեմ ... [nerets'eq khndrem ...]
I'm looking for ...	Ես փնտրում եմ ... [yes pntrum am ...]

the subway	մետրո [metr'o]
my hotel	իմ հյուրանոցը [im hyuran'otsy]
the movie theater	կինոթատրոն [kinotatr'on]
a taxi stand	տաքսիների կայան [taxiner'i kay'an]

an ATM	բանկոմատ [bankom'at]
a foreign exchange office	արժույթի փոխանակման կետ [arzhuyt'i pvokhanakm'an ket]
an internet café	ինտերնետ-սրճարան [intern'et-srchar'an]
... street	... փողոցը [... pogh'otsy]
this place	այս տեղը ['ays t'eghy]

Do you know where ... is?	Դուք գիտե՞ք՝ որտեղ է գտնվում ...: [duq git'eq vort'egh e gtnv'um ...?]
Which street is this?	Ինչպե՞ս է կոչվում այս փողոցը: [inchp'es e kochv'um ays pvogh'otsy?]

Show me where we are right now.	Ցույց տվեք՝ որտեղ ենք մենք հիմա: [tsuyts tveq vort'egh enq menq him'a]
Can I get there on foot?	Ես կհասնե՞մ այնտեղ ոտքով: [yes khasn'em aynt'egh votq'ov?]
Do you have a map of the city?	Դուք ունե՞ք քաղաքի քարտեզը: [duq un'eq qagh'aqi qart'ezy?]

How much is a ticket to get in?	Որքա՞ն արժե մուտքի տոմսը: [vorq'an arzh'e mutqi t'omsy?]
Can I take pictures here?	Այստեղ կարելի՞ է լուսանկարել: [ayst'egh karel'i e lusankar'el?]
Are you open?	Դուք բա՞ց եք: [duq b'ats eq?]

When do you open?

Ժամը քանիսի՞ն եք դուք բացվում:
[zh'amy qanis'in eq duq batsv'um?]

When do you close?

Մինչև ո՞ր ժամն եք աշխատում:
[minch'ev vor zhamn eq ashkhat'um?]

Money

money	փող [pogh]
cash	կանխիկ դրամ [kankh'ik dram]
paper money	թղթադրամ [tghtadr'am]
loose change	մանրադրամ [manradr'am]
check | change | tip	հաշիվ | մանր | թեյավճար [hash'iv | manr | tyeyavch'ar]

credit card	կրեդիտ քարտ [kred'it qart]
wallet	դրամապանակ [dramapan'ak]
to buy	գնել [gnel]
to pay	վճարել [vchar'el]
fine	տուգանք [tug'anq]
free	անվճար [anvch'ar]

Where can I buy ...?	Որտե՞ղ կարող եմ գնել ...: [vort'egh kar'ogh am gnel ...?]
Is the bank open now?	Բանկը հիմա բա՞ց է: [b'anky him'a bats e?]
When does it open?	Ժամը քանիսի՞ն է այն բացվում: [zh'amy qanis'in e 'ayn batsv'um?]
When does it close?	Մինչև ո՞ր ժամն է այն աշխատում: [minch'ev vor zhamn e 'ayn ashkhat'um?]

How much?	Ինչքա՞ն: [inchq'an?]
How much is this?	Սա ինչքա՞ն արժե: [sa inchq'an arzh'e?]
That's too expensive.	Դա չափազանց թանկ է: [da chapaz'ants tank e]

Excuse me, where do I pay?	Ներեցեք, որտե՞ղ է դրամարկղը: [nerets'eq, vort'egh e dram'arkghy?]
Check, please.	Հաշիվը, խնդրում եմ: [hash'ivy, khndrum em]

Can I pay by credit card? | Կարո՞ղ եմ վճարել քարտով:
[kar'ogh am vchar'el qart'ov?]

Is there an ATM here? | Այստեղ բանկոմատ կա՞:
[ayst'egh bankom'at ka?]

I'm looking for an ATM. | Ինձ բանկոմատ է հարկավոր:
[indz bankom'at e harkav'or?]

I'm looking for a foreign exchange office. | Ես փնտրում եմ փոխանակման կետ:
[yes pntrum am pokhanakm'an ket]

I'd like to change ... | Ես ուզում եմ փոխանակել ...
[yes uz'um am pokhanak'el ...]

What is the exchange rate? | Ասացեք, խնդրեմ, փոխարժեքը:
[asats'eq, khndrem, pokharzh'eqy?]

Do you need my passport? | Ձեզ պե՞տք է իմ անձնագիրը:
[dzez petq e im andznag'iry?]

Time

What time is it?	Ժամը քանի՞սն է: [zh'amy qan'isn e?]
When?	Ե՞րբ: [yerb?]
At what time?	Ժամը քանիսի՞ն: [zh'amy qanis'in?]
now | later | after ...	հիմա | ավելի ուշ | ...ից հետո [him'a | avel'i ush | ...its het'o]
one o'clock	ցերեկվա ժամը մեկը [tserekv'a zh'amy m'eky]
one fifteen	մեկն անց տասնհինգ րոպե [mekn ants tasnh'ing rop'e]
one thirty	մեկն անց կես [m'ekn ants kes]
one forty-five	երկուսին տասնհինգ պակաս [yerkus'in tasnh'ing pak'as]
one | two | three	մեկ | երկու | երեք [mek | yerk'u | yer'ek]
four | five | six	չորս | հինգ | վեց [chors | hing | vets]
seven | eight | nine	յոթ | ութ | ինը [yot | ut | 'iny]
ten | eleven | twelve	տաս | տասնմեկ | տասներկու [tas | tasnm'ek | tasnerk'u]
in ...	...ից [...its]
five minutes	հինգ րոպե [hing rop'e]
ten minutes	տաս րոպե [tas rop'e]
fifteen minutes	տասնհինգ րոպե [tasnh'ing rop'e]
twenty minutes	քսան րոպե [qsan rop'e]
half an hour	կես ժամ [kes zham]
an hour	մեկ ժամ [mek zham]

in the morning	առավոտյան [aravoty'an]
early in the morning	վաղ առավոտյան [vagh aravoty'an]
this morning	այսօր առավոտյան [ays'or aravoty'an]
tomorrow morning	վաղն առավոտյան [v'aghn aravoty'an]
at noon	ճաշին [chash'in]
in the afternoon	ճաշից հետո [chash'its het'o]
in the evening	երեկոյան [yerekoy'an]
tonight	այսօր երեկոյան [ays'or yerekoy'an]
at night	գիշերը [gish'ery]
yesterday	երեկ [yer'ek]
today	այսօր [ays'or]
tomorrow	վաղը [v'aghy]
the day after tomorrow	վաղը չէ մյուս օրը [v'aghy che my'us 'ory]
What day is it today?	Շաբաթվա ի՞նչ օր է այսօր: [shabatv'a inch or e ays'or?]
It's ...	Այսօր ... է: [ays'or ... e]
Monday	երկուշաբթի [yerkushabt'i]
Tuesday	երեքշաբթի [yerekshabt'i]
Wednesday	չորեքշաբթի [choreqshabt'i]
Thursday	հինգշաբթի [hingshabt'i]
Friday	ուրբաթ [urb'at]
Saturday	շաբաթ [shab'at]
Sunday	կիրակի [kirak'i]

Greetings. Introductions

Hello.
Բարև Ձեզ:
[bar'ev dzez]

Pleased to meet you.
Ուրախ եմ Ձեզ հետ ծանոթանալու:
[ur'akh am dzez het tsanotanal'u]

Me too.
Նմանապես:
[nmanap'es]

I'd like you to meet ...
Ծանոթացեք։ Սա ... է:
[tsanotats'ek. sa ... e]

Nice to meet you.
Շատ հաճելի է:
[shat hacheľi e]

How are you?
Ինչպե՞ս եք: Ինչպե՞ս են ձեր գործերը:
[inchp'es eq? inchp'es en dzer gorts'ery?]

My name is ...
Իմ անունը ... է:
[im an'uny ... e]

His name is ...
Նրա անունը ... է:
[nra an'uny ... e]

Her name is ...
Նրա անունը ... է:
[nra an'uny ... e]

What's your name?
Ձեր անունն ի՞նչ է:
[dzer an'unn inch e?]

What's his name?
Ի՞նչ է նրա անունը:
[inch e nra an'uny?]

What's her name?
Ի՞նչ է նրա անունը:
[inch e nra an'uny?]

What's your last name?
Ի՞նչ է ձեր ազգանունը:
[inch e dzer azgan'uny?]

You can call me ...
Ասացեք ինձ ...
[asac'eq indz ...]

Where are you from?
Որտեղի՞ց եք դուք:
[vortegh'its eq duq?]

I'm from ...
Ես ...ից եմ:
[yes ...its am]

What do you do for a living?
Որտե՞ղ եք աշխատում:
[vort'egh eq ashkhat'um?]

Who is this?
Ո՞վ է սա:
[ov e sa?]

Who is he?
Ո՞վ է նա:
[ov e na?]

Who is she?
Ո՞վ է նա:
[ov e na?]

Who are they?
Ո՞վ են նրանք:
[ov en nr'ank?]

This is ...	Սա ...ն է: [sa ...n e]
my friend (masc.)	իմ ընկեր [im ynk'er]
my friend (fem.)	իմ ընկերուհի [im ynkeruh'i]
my husband	իմ ամուսին [im amus'in]
my wife	իմ կին [im kin]
my father	իմ հայր [im hayr]
my mother	իմ մայր [im mayr]
my brother	իմ եղբայր [im yeghb'ayr]
my sister	իմ քույր [im quyr]
my son	իմ որդի [im vord'i]
my daughter	իմ դուստր [im dustr]
This is our son.	Սա մեր որդին է: [sa mer vord'in e]
This is our daughter.	Սա մեր դուստրն է: [sa mer d'ustrn e]
These are my children.	Սրանք իմ երեխաներն են: [srank im yerekhan'ern en]
These are our children.	Սրանք մեր երեխաներն են: [srank mer yerekhan'ern en]

Farewells

Good bye! — Ցտեսություն։
[tstesuty'un!]

Bye! (inform.) — Հաջող։
[haj'ogh!]

See you tomorrow. — Մինչ վաղը։
[minch v'aghy]

See you soon. — Մինչ հանդիպում։
[minch handip'um]

See you at seven. — Կհանդիպենք ժամը յոթին։
[khandip'enk zh'amy yot'in]

Have fun! — Զվարճացեք։
[zvarchats'eq!]

Talk to you later. — Հետո կխոսենք։
[het'o kkhos'enq]

Have a nice weekend. — Հաջող հանգստյան օրեր եմ ցանկանում։
[haj'ogh hangsty'an or'er am tsankan'um]

Good night. — Բարի գիշեր։
[bar'i gish'er]

It's time for me to go. — Գնալուս ժամանակն է։
[gnal'us zhaman'akn e]

I have to go. — Ես պետք է գնամ։
[yes petq e gnam]

I will be right back. — Ես հիմա կվերադառնամ։
[yes him'a kveradarn'am]

It's late. — Արդեն ուշ է։
[ard'en 'ush e]

I have to get up early. — Ես պետք է վաղ արթնանամ։
[yes petq e vagh artnan'am]

I'm leaving tomorrow. — Ես վաղը մեկնում եմ։
[yes v'aghy mekn'um am]

We're leaving tomorrow. — Մենք վաղը մեկնում ենք։
[menq v'aghy mekn'um enq]

Have a nice trip! — Բարի ճանապա~րհ։
[bar'i chanap'arh!]

It was nice meeting you. — Հաճելի էր Ձեզ հետ ծանոթանալ։
[hachel'i er dzez het tsanotan'al]

It was nice talking to you. — Հաճելի էր Ձեզ հետ շփվել։
[hachel'i er dzez het shpv'el]

Thanks for everything. — Շնորհակալություն ամեն ինչի համար։
[shnorhakaluty'un am'en inch'i ham'ar]

I had a very good time.	Ես հյակապ անցկացրեցի ժամանակը:
	[yes hoyak'ap antskatsrets'i zhaman'aky]
We had a very good time.	Մենք հյակապ անցկացրեցինք ժամանակը:
	[menq hoyak'ap antskatsrets'inq zhaman'aky]
It was really great.	Ամեն ինչ հյակապ էր:
	[am'en inch hoyak'ap er]
I'm going to miss you.	Ես կկարոտեմ:
	[yes kkarot'em]
We're going to miss you.	Մենք կկարոտենք:
	[menq kkarot'enq]
Good luck!	Հաջողությո՜ւն: Մնաք բարո՜վ:
	[hajoghuty'un! mnaq baro'v!]
Say hi to …	Բարեք …ին:
	[barev'eq …in]

Foreign language

I don't understand.	Ես չեմ հասկանում: [yes chem haskan'um]
Write it down, please.	Խնդրում եմ, գրեք դա: [khndrum em, greq da]
Do you speak ...?	Դուք գիտե՞ք ...: [duq git'eq ...?]

I speak a little bit of ...	Ես գիտեմ մի քիչ ... [yes git'em mi qich ...]
English	անգլերեն [angler'en]
Turkish	թուրքերեն [turker'en]
Arabic	արաբերեն [araber'en]
French	ֆրանսերեն [franser'en]

German	գերմաներեն [germaner'en]
Italian	իտալերեն [italer'en]
Spanish	իսպաներեն [ispaner'en]
Portuguese	պորտուգալերեն [portugaler'en]
Chinese	չիներեն [chiner'en]
Japanese	ճապոներեն [chaponer'en]

Can you repeat that, please.	Կրկնեք, խնդրեմ: [krkneq, khndrem]
I understand.	Ես հասկանում եմ: [yes haskan'um am]
I don't understand.	Ես չեմ հասկանում: [yes chem haskan'um]
Please speak more slowly.	Խոսեք դանդաղ, խնդրում եմ: [khos'eq dand'agh, khndrum em]

Is that correct? (Am I saying it right?)	Սա ճի՞շտ է: [sa chisht e?]
What is this? (What does this mean?)	Ի՞նչ է սա: [inch e sa?]

Apologies

Excuse me, please.

Ներեցեք, խնդրեմ:
[nerets'eq, khndrem]

I'm sorry.

Ցավում եմ:
[tsav'um am]

I'm really sorry.

Շատ ափսոս:
[shat aps'os]

Sorry, it's my fault.

Իմ մեղավորությունն է:
[im meghavoruty'unn e]

My mistake.

Իմ սխալն է:
[im skh'aln e]

May I ...?

Ես կարո՞ղ եմ ...:
[yes kar'ogh am ...?]

Do you mind if I ...?

Դեմ չե՞ք լինի, եթե ես ...:
[dem cheq lini, yet'e yes ...?]

It's OK.

Սարսափելի ոչինչ չկա:
[sarsap'eli voch'inch chka]

It's all right.

Ամեն ինչ կարգին է:
[am'en inch karg'in e]

Don't worry about it.

Մի անհանգստացեք:
[mi anhangstats'eq]

Agreement

Yes.	Այո: [ay'o]
Yes, sure.	Այո, իհարկե: [ay'o, ih'arke]
OK (Good!)	Լավ: [lav!]
Very well.	Շատ լավ: [shat lav]
Certainly!	Իհարկե: [ih'arke]
I agree.	Ես համաձայն եմ: [yes hamadz'ayn am]
That's correct.	Ճիշտ է: [chisht e]
That's right.	Ճիշտ է: [chisht e]
You're right.	Դուք իրավացի եք: [duq iravats'i eq]
I don't mind.	Ես չեմ առարկում: [yes chem arark'um]
Absolutely right.	Բացարձակ ճիշտ է: [batsardz'ak ch'isht e]
It's possible.	Հնարավոր է: [hnarav'or e]
That's a good idea.	Լավ միտք է: [lav mitq e]
I can't say no.	Չեմ կարող մերժել: [chem kar'ogh merzh'el]
I'd be happy to.	Ուրախ կլինեմ: [ur'akh klin'em]
With pleasure.	Հաճույքով: [hachuyq'ov]

Refusal. Expressing doubt

No.	Ոչ: [voch]
Certainly not.	Իհարկե, ոչ: [ih'arke, voch]
I don't agree.	Ես համաձայն չեմ: [yes hamadz'ayn chem]
I don't think so.	Ես այդպես չեմ կարծում: [yes ayes chem karts'um]
It's not true.	Սուտ է: [sut e]
You are wrong.	Դուք իրավացի չեք: [duq iravats'i cheq]
I think you are wrong.	Կարծում եմ` իրավացի չեք: [karts'um am iravats'i cheq]
I'm not sure.	Համոզված չեմ: [hamozv'ats chem]
It's impossible.	Անհնար է: [anhn'ar e]
Nothing of the kind (sort)!	Ո՛չ մի նման բան: [voch mi nman ban]
The exact opposite.	Հակառակը: [hakar'aky!]
I'm against it.	Ես դեմ եմ: [yes dem am]
I don't care.	Ինձ միևնույն է: [indz mievn'uyn e]
I have no idea.	Գաղափար չունեմ: [gaghap'ar chun'em]
I doubt that.	Կասկածում եմ, որ այդպես է: [kaskats'um am, vor aydp'es e]
Sorry, I can't.	Ներեցեք, չեմ կարող: [nerets'eq, chem kar'ogh]
Sorry, I don't want to.	Ներեցեք, չեմ ուզում: [nerets'eq, chem uz'um]
Thank you, but I don't need this.	Շնորհակալություն, ինձ պետք չէ: [shnorhakaluty'un, indz petq che]
It's late.	Արդեն ուշ է: [ard'en 'ush e]

I have to get up early.

Ես պետք է վաղ արթնանամ:
[yes petq e vagh artnan'am]

I don't feel well.

Ես ինձ վատ եմ զգում:
[indz vat am zgum]

Expressing gratitude

Thank you.

Շնորհակալություն։
[shnorhakaluty'un]

Thank you very much.

Շատ շնորհակալ եմ։
[shat shnorhak'al am]

I really appreciate it.

Շատ շնորհակալ եմ։
[shat shnorhak'al am]

I'm really grateful to you.

Շնորհակալ եմ։
[shnorhak'al am]

We are really grateful to you.

Շնորհակալ ենք։
[shnorhak'al enq]

Thank you for your time.

Շնորհակալություն, որ ծախսեցիք
ձեր ժամանակը։
[shnorhakaluty'un, vor tsakhsets'ik
dzer zhaman'aky]

Thanks for everything.

Շնորհակալություն ամեն ինչի համար։
[shnorhakaluty'un am'en inch'i ham'ar]

Thank you for ...

Շնորհակալություն ... համար։
[shnorhakaluty'un ... ham'ar]

your help

ձեր օգնության
[dzer ognuty'an]

a nice time

լավ ժամանցի
[lav zhamants'i]

a wonderful meal

հոյակապ ուտեստների
[hoyak'ap utestner'i]

a pleasant evening

հաճելի երեկոյի
[hachel'i erekoy'i]

a wonderful day

հիանալի օրվա
[hianal'i orv'a]

an amazing journey

հետաքրքիր էքսկուրսիայի
[hetaqrq'ir eqskursiay'i]

Don't mention it.

Չարժե։
[charzh'e]

You are welcome.

Չարժե։
[charzh'e]

Any time.

Միշտ խնդրեմ։
[misht khndrem]

My pleasure.

Ուրախ էի օգնելու։
[ur'akh ei ognel'u]

Forget it. It's alright.   **Մոռացեք:**
[morats'eq]

Don't worry about it.   **Մի անհանգստացեք:**
[mi anhangstats'eq]

Congratulations. Best wishes

Congratulations!

Շնորհավորում եմ:
[shnorhavor'um am!]

Happy birthday!

Շնորհավոր ծննդյան օրը:
[shnorhav'or tsnndy'an 'ory!]

Merry Christmas!

Շնորհավոր Սուրբ ծնունդը:
[shnorhav'or surb tsnund!]

Happy New Year!

Շնորհավոր Ամանորը:
[shnorhav'or aman'or!]

Happy Easter!

Շնորհավոր Զատիկ:
[shnorhav'or zat'ik!]

Happy Hanukkah!

Ուրախ Հանուկա:
[ur'akh h'anuka!]

I'd like to propose a toast.

Ես կենաց ունեմ:
[yes ken'ats un'em]

Cheers!

Ձեր առողջության կենացը:
[dzer aroghjuty'an ken'atsy!]

Let's drink to …!

Խմենք … համար:
[khmenq … ham'ar!]

To our success!

Մեր հաջողության կենացը:
[mer hajoghuty'an ken'atsy!]

To your success!

Ձեր հաջողության կենացը:
[dzer hajoghuty'an ken'atsy!]

Good luck!

Հաջողություն:
[hajoghuty'un!]

Have a nice day!

Հաճելի օր եմ ցանկանում:
[hachel'i 'or am tsankan'um!]

Have a good holiday!

Հաճելի հանգիստ եմ ցանկանում:
[hachel'l hang'ist am tsankan'um!]

Have a safe journey!

Բարի ճանապարհ:
[bar'i chanap'arh!]

I hope you get better soon!

Շուտ ապաքինում եմ ցանկանում:
[shut apaqin'um am cankan'um!]

Socializing

Why are you sad?

Ինչո՞ւ եք տխրել:
[inxh'u eq tkhrel?]

Smile! Cheer up!

Ժպտացե՛ք!
[zhptatsy'ek!]

Are you free tonight?

Դուք զբաղվա՞ծ եք այսոր երեկոյան:
[duq zbaghv'ats eq ays'or yerekoy'an?]

May I offer you a drink?

Կարո՞ղ եմ առաջարկել
ձեզ որևէ ըմպելիք:
[kar'ogh am arajark'el
dzez vorev'e ympel'iq?]

Would you like to dance?

Չե՞ք ցանկանա պարել:
[cheq tsankan'a par'el?]

Let's go to the movies.

Գնա՛նք կինոթատրոն:
[gnanq kinotatr'on?]

May I invite you to ...?

Կարո՞ղ եմ հրավիրել ձեզ ...:
[kar'ogh am hravir'el dzez ...?]

a restaurant

ռեստորան
[rrestor'an]

the movies

կինոթատրոն
[kinotatr'on]

the theater

թատրոն
[tatr'on]

go for a walk

զբոսանքի
[zbosanq'i]

At what time?

Ժամը քանիսի՞ն:
[zh'amy qanis'in?]

tonight

այսոր երեկոյան
[ays'or yerekoy'an]

at six

ժամը վեցին
[zh'amy vec'in]

at seven

ժամը յոթին
[zh'amy yot'in]

at eight

ժամը ութին
[zh'amy out'in]

at nine

ժամը իննին
[zh'amy inn'in]

Do you like it here?

Ձեզ այստեղ դո՞ւր է գալիս:
[dzez ayst'egh dur e gal'is?]

Are you here with someone?

Դուք այստեղ ինչ-որ մեկի հե՞տ եք:
[duq ayst'egh inch-vor mek'i het eq?]

I'm with my friend.

Ես ընկերոջս /ընկերուհուս/ հետ եմ:
[yes ynker'ojs /ynkeruh'us/ het am]

I'm with my friends.

Ես ընկերներիս հետ եմ:
[yes ynkerner'is het am]

No, I'm alone.

Ես մենակ եմ:
[yes men'ak am]

Do you have a boyfriend?

Դու ընկեր ունե՞ս:
[du ynk'er un'es?]

I have a boyfriend.

Ես ընկեր ունեմ:
[yes ynk'er un'em]

Do you have a girlfriend?

Դու ընկերուհի ունե՞ս:
[du ynkeruh'i un'es?]

I have a girlfriend.

Ես ընկերուհի ունեմ:
[yes ynkeruh'i un'em]

Can I see you again?

Մենք դեռ կհանդիպե՞նք:
[menq der khandip'enq?]

Can I call you?

Կարո՞ղ եմ քեզ զանգահարել:
[kar'ogh am qez zangahar'el?]

Call me. (Give me a call.)

Կզանգես:
[kzang'es]

What's your number?

Ո՞նց է համարդ
[vonts e ham'ard?]

I miss you.

Ես կարոտում եմ քեզ:
[yes karot'um am qez]

You have a beautiful name.

Դուք շատ գեղեցիկ անուն ունեք:
[duq shat geghets'ik an'un un'eq]

I love you.

Ես սիրում եմ քեզ:
[yes sir'um am qez]

Will you marry me?

Արի՛ ամուսնանանք:
[ar'i amusnan'anq]

You're kidding!

Դուք կատակում եք:
[duq katak'um eq!]

I'm just kidding.

Ես ուղղակի կատակում եմ:
[yes ughghak'i katak'um am]

Are you serious?

Դուք լո՞ւրջ եք ասում:
[duq l'urj eq as'um?]

I'm serious.

Ես լուրջ եմ ասում:
[yes lurj am as'um]

Really?!

Իրո՞ք:
[ir'oq?!]

It's unbelievable!

Դա անհավանական է:
[da anhavanak'an e!]

I don't believe you.

Ես ձեզ չեմ հավատում:
[yes dzez chem havat'um]

I can't.

Ես չեմ կարող:
[yes chem kar'ogh]

I don't know.

Ես չգիտեմ:
[yes chgit'em]

I don't understand you.	Ես ձեզ չեմ հասկանում: [yes dzez chem haskan'um]
Please go away.	Հեռացեք, խնդրում եմ: [herats'ek, khndrum em]
Leave me alone!	Ինձ հանգ՛ ´ստ թողեք: [indz hang'ist togh'eq]

I can't stand him.	Ես նրան տանել չեմ կարողանում: [yes nran tan'el chem karoghan'um]
You are disgusting!	Դուք զզվելի եք: [duq zzvel'i eq!]
I'll call the police!	Ես ոստիկանություն կկանչեմ: [yes vostikanuty'un kkanch'em!]

Sharing impressions. Emotions

I like it.	Ինձ դա դուր է գալիս։ [indz da dur e gal'is]
Very nice.	Հաճելի է։ [hachel'i e]
That's great!	Հրաշալի է։ [hrashal'i e!]
It's not bad.	Վատ չէ։ [vat che]
I don't like it.	Սա ինձ դուր է գալիս։ [indz dur e gal'is]
It's not good.	Դա լավ չի։ [da lav chi]
It's bad.	Դա վատ է։ [da vat e]
It's very bad.	Դա շատ վատ է։ [da shat vat e]
It's disgusting.	Զզվելի է։ [zzvel'i e]
I'm happy.	Ես երջանիկ եմ։ [yes yerjan'ik am]
I'm content.	Ես գոհ եմ։ [yes goh am]
I'm in love.	Ես սիրահարվել եմ։ [yes siraharv'el am]
I'm calm.	Ես հանգիստ եմ։ [yes hang'ist am]
I'm bored.	Ես ձանձրանում եմ։ [yes dzandzran'um am]
I'm tired.	Ես հոգնել եմ։ [yes hogn'el am]
I'm sad.	Ես տխուր եմ։ [yes tkhur am]
I'm frightened.	Ես վախեցած եմ։ [yes vakhets'ats am]
I'm angry.	Ես զայրանում եմ։ [yes zayran'um am]
I'm worried.	Ես անհանգստանում եմ։ [yes anhangstan'um am]
I'm nervous.	Ես ջղայնանում եմ։ [yes jghaynan'um am]

I'm jealous. (envious)

Ես նախանձում եմ:
[yes nakhandz'um am]

I'm surprised.

Ես զարմացած եմ:
[yes zarmats'ats am]

I'm perplexed.

Ես շփոթված եմ:
[yes shpvotv'ats am]

Problems. Accidents

I've got a problem.

Ես խնդիր ունեմ:
[yes khndir un'em]

We've got a problem.

Մենք խնդիրներ ունենք:
[menq khndirn'er un'enq]

I'm lost.

Ես մոլորվել եմ:
[yes molorv'el am]

I missed the last bus (train).

Ես ուշացել եմ վերջին ավտոբուսից
(գնացքից):
[yes ushats'el am verj'in avtob'usits
(gnatsq'its)]

I don't have any money left.

Ինձ մոտ դրամ ընդհանրապես
չի մնացել:
[indz mot dram yndhanrap'es
chi mnats'el]

I've lost my ...

Ես կորցրել եմ ...
[yes kortsr'el am ...]

Someone stole my ...

Ինձ մոտից գողացել են ...
[indz mot'its goghats'el en ...]

passport

անձնագիրը
[andznag'iry]

wallet

դրամապանակը
[dramapan'aky]

papers

փաստաթղթերը
[pastatght'ery]

ticket

տոմսը
[t'omsy]

money

փողը
[p'oghy]

handbag

պայուսակը
[payus'aky]

camera

ֆոտոապարատը
[fotoapar'aty]

laptop

նոութբուքը
[noteb'ooky]

tablet computer

պլանշետը
[plansh'ety]

mobile phone

հեռախոսը
[herakh'osy]

Help me!

Oգնեցե՜ք:
[ognets'eq!]

What's happened?

Ի՞նչ է պատահել:
[inch e patah'el?]

fire	հրդեհ [hrdeh]
shooting	կրակոց [krak'ots]
murder	սպանություն [spanuty'un]
explosion	պայթյուն [payty'un]
fight	կռիվ [kriv]

Call the police!	Ոստիկանություն կանչեք: [vostikanuty'un kanch'eq!]
Please hurry up!	Արագացրեք, խնդրում եմ: [aragats'req, khndrum em!]
I'm looking for the police station.	Ես փնտրում եմ ոստիկանության բաժին [yes pntrum am vostikanuty'an bazh'in]
I need to make a call.	Ինձ պետք է զանգահարել: [indz petq e zangahar'el]
May I use your phone?	Կարո՞ղ եմ զանգահարել: [kar'ogh am zangahar'el?]

I've been ...	Ինձ ... [indz ...]
mugged	կողոպտել են [koghopt'el en]
robbed	թալանել են [talan'el en]
raped	բռնաբարել են [brnabar'el en]
attacked (beaten up)	ծեծել են [tsets'el en]

Are you all right?	Ձեզ հետ ամեն ինչ կարգի՞ն է: [dzez het am'en inch karg'in e?]
Did you see who it was?	Դուք տեսե՞լ եք, ով էր նա: [duq tes'el eq, ov er na?]
Would you be able to recognize the person?	Կարո՞ղ եք նրան ճանաչել: [kar'ogh eq nran chanach'el?]
Are you sure?	Համոզվա՞ծ եք: [hamozv'ats eq?]

Please calm down.	Խնդրում եմ, հանգստացեք: [khndrum em, hangstats'eq]
Take it easy!	Հանգիստ: [hang'ist!]
Don't worry!	Մի անհանգստացեք: [mi anhangstats'eq]
Everything will be fine.	Ամեն ինչ լավ կլինի: [am'en inch lav klin'i]
Everything's all right.	Ամեն ինչ կարգին է: [am'en inch karg'in e]

Come here, please.

Մոտեցեք, խնդրեմ:
[motets'eq, khndrem]

I have some questions for you.

Ես ձեզ մի քանի հարց ունեմ տալու:
[yes dzez mi qan'i harts un'em tal'u]

Wait a moment, please.

Սպասեք, խնդրեմ:
[spas'eq, khndrem]

Do you have any I.D.?

Դուք փաստաթղթեր ունե՞ք:
[duq pastatght'er un'eq?]

Thanks. You can leave now.

Շնորհակալություն:
Դուք կարող եք գնալ:
[shnorhakaluty'un.
duq kar'ogh eq gnal]

Hands behind your head!

Ձեռքերը գլխի հետև՛:
[dzerk'ery glkhi het'ev!]

You're under arrest!

Դուք ձերբակալվա՛ծ եք:
[duq dzerbakalv'ats eq!]

Health problems

Please help me.	Oգնեցեք, խնդրում եմ: [ognets'eq, khndrum em]
I don't feel well.	Ես ինձ վատ եմ զգում: [yes indz vat am zgum]
My husband doesn't feel well.	Իմ ամուսինն իրեն վատ է զգում: [im amus'inn ir'en vat e zgum]
My son ...	Իմ որդին ... [im vord'in ...]
My father ...	Իմ հայրն ... [im hayrn ...]
My wife doesn't feel well.	Իմ կինն իրեն վատ է զգում: [im kinn ir'en vat e zgum]
My daughter ...	Իմ դուստրն ... [im dustrn ...]
My mother ...	Իմ մայրն ... [im mayrn ...]
I've got a ...	Իմ ... ցավում է: [im ... tsav'um e]
headache	գլուխը [gl'ukhy]
sore throat	կոկորդը [kok'ordy]
stomach ache	փորը [p'ory]
toothache	ատամը [at'amy]
I feel dizzy.	Գլուխս պտտվում է: [glukhs pttvum e]
He has a fever.	Նա ջերմություն ունի: [na jermuty'un un'i]
She has a fever.	Նա ջերմություն ունի: [na jermuty'un un'i]
I can't breathe.	Ես չեմ կարողանում շնչել: [yes chem karoghan'um shnch'el]
I'm short of breath.	Խեղդվում եմ: [kheghdv'um am]
I am asthmatic.	Ես աստմահար եմ: [yes astmah'ar am]
I am diabetic.	Ես շաքարախտ ունեմ: [yes shakar'akht un'em]

I can't sleep.	Ես անքնություն ունեմ։ [yes anknuty'un un'em]
food poisoning	սննդային թունավորում [snnday'in tunavor'um]

It hurts here.	Այստեղ է ցավում։ [ayst'egh e tsav'um]
Help me!	Օգնեցե՜ք։ [ognets'eq!]
I am here!	Ես այստեղ եմ։ [yes ayst'egh am!]
We are here!	Մենք այստեղ ենք։ [menq ayst'egh enq!]
Get me out of here!	Հանեք ինձ։ [khan'ek indz!]
I need a doctor.	Ինձ բժիշկ է պետք։ [indz bzhishk e petq]
I can't move.	Ես չեմ կարողանում շարժվել։ [yes chem karoghan'um sharzhv'el]
I can't move my legs.	Ես չեմ զգում ոտքերս։ [yes chem zgum votq'ers]

I have a wound.	Ես վիրավոր եմ։ [yes virav'or am]
Is it serious?	Լո՞ւրջ։ [lurj?]
My documents are in my pocket.	Իմ փաստաթղթերը գրպանումս են։ [im pastatght'ery grpan'ums en]
Calm down!	Հանգստացեք։ [hangstats'eq!]
May I use your phone?	Կարո՞ղ եմ զանգահարել։ [kar'ogh am zangahar'el?]

Call an ambulance!	Շտապ օգնություն կանչեք։ [shtap ognuty'un kanch'eq!]
It's urgent!	Սա շտապ է։ [sa shtap e!]
It's an emergency!	Սա շատ շտապ է։ [sa shat shtap e!]
Please hurry up!	Արագացրեք, խնդրում եմ։ [aragatsr'eq, khndrum em!]
Would you please call a doctor?	Բժիշկ կանչեք, խնդրում եմ։ [bzhishk kanch'eq, khndrum em]
Where is the hospital?	Ասացեք, որտե՞ղ է հիվանդանոցը։ [asats'eq, vort'egh e hivandan'otsy?]

How are you feeling?	Ինչպե՞ս եք ձեզ զգում։ [inchp'es eq dzez zgum?]
Are you all right?	Ձեզ հետ ամեն ինչ կարգի՞ն է։ [dzez het am'en inch karg'in e?]
What's happened?	Ի՞նչ է պատահել։ [inch e patah'el?]

I feel better now.

Ես արդեն ինձ լավ եմ զգում:
[indz lav am zgum]

It's OK.

Ամեն ինչ կարգին է:
[am'en inch karg'in e]

It's all right.

Ամեն ինչ լավ է:
[am'en inch l'av e]

At the pharmacy

pharmacy (drugstore)	դեղատուն [deghat'un]
24-hour pharmacy	շուրջօրյա դեղատուն [shurjor'ya deghat'un]
Where is the closest pharmacy?	Որտե՞ղ է մոտակա դեղատունը: [vort'egh e motak'a deghat'uny?]
Is it open now?	Այն հիմա բա՞ց է: [ayn him'a bats e?]
At what time does it open?	Ժամը քանիսի՞ն է այն բացվում: [zh'amy qanis'in e 'ayn batsv'um?]
At what time does it close?	Մինչև ո՞ր ժամն է այն աշխատում: [minch'ev vor zhamn e 'ayn ashkhat'um?]
Is it far?	Դա հեռո՞ւ է: [da her'u e?]
Can I get there on foot?	Ես կհասնե՞մ այնտեղ ոտքով: [yes khasn'em aynt'egh votq'ov?]
Can you show me on the map?	Ցույց տվեք ինձ քարտեզի վրա, խնդրում եմ: [tsuyts tveq indz qartez'i vra, khndrum am]
Please give me something for ...	Տվեք ինձ ինչ-որ բան ... համար: [tveq indz inch-v'or ban ... ham'ar]
a headache	գլխացավի [glkhatsav'i]
a cough	հազի [haz'i]
a cold	մրսածության [mrsatsuty'an]
the flu	հարբուխի [harbukh'i]
a fever	ջերմության [jermuty'an]
a stomach ache	փորացավի [poratsav'i]
nausea	սրտխառնոցի [srtkharnots'i]
diarrhea	լուծի [luts'i]
constipation	փորկապության [porkaputy'an]

pain in the back

մեջքի ցավ
[mejk'i tsav]

chest pain

կրծքի ցավ
[krtski tsav]

side stitch

կողացավ
[koghats'av]

abdominal pain

փորացավ
[porats'av]

pill

հաբ
[hab]

ointment, cream

քսուք, կրեմ
[ksuk, krem]

syrup

օշարակ
[oshar'ak]

spray

սփրեյ
[spr'ay]

drops

կաթիլներ
[katiln'er]

You need to go to the hospital.

Դուք պետք է հիվանդանոց գնաք:
[duq petq e hivandan'ots gna]

health insurance

ապահովագրություն
[apahovagruty'un]

prescription

դեղատոմս
[deghat'oms]

insect repellant

միջատների դեմ միջոց
[mijatner'i dem mij'ots]

Band Aid

լեյկոսպեղանի
[leykospeghan'i]

The bare minimum

Excuse me, ...	Ներեցեք, ... [nerets'eq, ...]
Hello.	Բարև Ձեզ: [bar'ev dzez]
Thank you.	Շնորհակալություն: [shnorhakaluty'un]
Good bye.	Ցտեսություն: [tstesuty'un]
Yes.	Այո: [ay'o]
No.	Ոչ: [voch]
I don't know.	Ես չգիտեմ: [yes chgit'em]
Where? | Where to? | When?	Ո՞րտեղ: Ո՞ւր: Ե՞րբ: [vort'egh? ur? yerb?]

I need ...	Ինձ հարկավոր է ... [indz harkav'or e ...]
I want ...	Ես ուզում եմ ... [yes uz'um em ...]
Do you have ...?	Դուք ունե՞ք ...: [duq un'eq ...?]
Is there a ... here?	Այստեղ կա՞ ...: [ayst'egh ka ...?]
May I ...?	Ես կարո՞ղ եմ ...: [yes kar'ogh em ...?]
..., please (polite request)	Խնդրում եմ [khndrum em]

I'm looking for ...	Ես փնտրում եմ ... [yes pntrum am ...]
restroom	զուգարան [zugar'an]
ATM	բանկոմատ [bankom'at]
pharmacy (drugstore)	դեղատուն [deghat'un]
hospital	հիվանդանոց [hivandan'ots]
police station	ոստիկանության բաժանմունք [vostikanuty'an bazhanm'unq]
subway	մետրո [metr'o]

taxi	տաքսի [tax'i]
train station	կայարան [kayar'an]

My name is ...	Իմ անունը ... է: [im an'uny ... e]
What's your name?	Ձեր անունն ի՞նչ է: [dzer an'unn inch e?]
Could you please help me?	Օգնեցեք ինձ, խնդրեմ: [ognets'eq indz, khndrem]
I've got a problem.	Ես խնդիր ունեմ: [yes khndir un'em]
I don't feel well.	Ես ինձ վատ եմ զգում: [yes indz vat am zgum]
Call an ambulance!	Շտապ օգնություն կանչեք: [shtap ognuty'un kanch'eq!]
May I make a call?	Կարո՞ղ եմ զանգահարել: [kar'ogh am zangahar'el?]

I'm sorry.	Ներեցեք [nerets'eq]
You're welcome.	Խնդրեմ [kndrem]

I, me	ես [yes]
you (inform.)	դու [du]
he	նա [na]
she	նա [na]
they (masc.)	նրանք [nrank]
they (fem.)	նրանք [nrank]
we	մենք [menq]
you (pl)	դուք [duq]
you (sg, form.)	Դուք [duq]

ENTRANCE	ՄՈՒՏՔ [mutq]
EXIT	ԵԼՔ [yelq]
OUT OF ORDER	ՉԻ ԱՇԽԱՏՈՒՄ [chi ashkhat'um]
CLOSED	ՓԱԿ Է [pak e]

OPEN   ԲԱՑ Է
          [bats e]

FOR WOMEN   ԿԱՆԱՆՑ ՀԱՄԱՐ
          [kan'ants ham'ar]

FOR MEN   ՏՂԱՄԱՐԴԿԱՆՑ ՀԱՄԱՐ
          [tghamardk'ants ham'ar]

CONCISE
DICTIONARY

This section contains more
than 1,500 useful words
arranged alphabetically.
The dictionary includes a lot
of gastronomic terms and
will be helpful when ordering
food at a restaurant or buying
groceries

T&P Books Publishing

DICTIONARY CONTENTS

T&P Books Publishing

T&P Books Publishing

time	ժամանակ	[ʒamaˈnak]
hour	ժամ	[ʒam]
half an hour	կես ժամ	[kes ˈʒam]
minute	րոպե	[roˈpɛ]
second	վայրկյան	[vajrˈkian]
today (adv)	այսոր	[ajˈsor]
tomorrow (adv)	վաղը	[ˈvahɪ]
yesterday (adv)	երեկ	[eˈrek]
Monday	երկուշաբթի	[erkuʃʌbˈti]
Tuesday	երեքշաբթի	[erekʃʌbˈti]
Wednesday	չորեքշաբթի	[tʃorekʃʌbˈti]
Thursday	հինգշաբթի	[inʃʌbˈti]
Friday	ուրբաթ	[urˈbat]
Saturday	շաբաթ	[ʃʌˈbat]
Sunday	կիրակի	[kiraˈki]
day	օր	[or]
working day	աշխատանքային օր	[aʃh ataŋkaˈjɪn ˈor]
public holiday	տոնական օր	[tonaˈkan ˈor]
weekend	շաբաթ, կիրակի	[ʃʌˈbat], [kiraˈki]
week	շաբաթ	[ʃʌˈbat]
last week (adv)	անցյալ շաբաթ	[anˈtsial ʃʌˈbat]
next week (adv)	հաջորդ շաբաթ	[aˈdʒort ˈorɪ]
sunrise	արևածագ	[arevaˈtsag]
sunset	մայրամուտ	[majraˈmut]
in the morning	առավոտյան	[aravoˈtian]
in the afternoon	ճաշից հետո	[tʃaˈʃits ɛˈto]
in the evening	երեկոյան	[erekoˈjan]
tonight (this evening)	այսոր երեկոյան	[ajˈsor erekoˈjan]
at night	գիշերը	[giˈʃerɪ]
midnight	կեսգիշեր	[kesgiˈʃer]
January	հունվար	[unˈvar]
February	փետրվար	[petrˈvar]
March	մարտ	[mart]
April	ապրիլ	[apˈril]
May	մայիս	[maˈjɪs]
June	հունիս	[uˈnis]

July	հուլիս	[u'lis]
August	օգոստոս	[ogos'tos]
September	սեպտեմբեր	[septem'ber]
October	հոկտեմբեր	[oktem'ber]
November	նոյեմբեր	[noem'ber]
December	դեկտեմբեր	[dektem'ber]

in spring	գարնանը	[gar'nanı]
in summer	ամռանը	[am'ranı]
in fall	աշնանը	[aʃ'nanı]
in winter	ձմռանը	[dzm'ranı]

month	ամիս	[a'mis]
season (summer, etc.)	սեզոն	[se'zon]
year	տարի	[ta'ri]
century	դար	[dar]

2. Numbers. Numerals

digit, figure	թիվ	[tiv]
number	թիվ	[tiv]
minus sign	մինուս	['minus]
plus sign	պլյուս	[plys]
sum, total	գումար	[gu'mar]

first (adj)	առաջին	[ara'dʒin]
second (adj)	երկրորդ	[erk'rord]
third (adj)	երրորդ	[er'rord]

0 zero	զրո	[zro]
1 one	մեկ	[mek]
2 two	երկու	[er'ku]
3 three	երեք	[e'rek]
4 four	չորս	[tʃors]

5 five	հինգ	[hiŋ]
6 six	վեց	[vets]
7 seven	յոթ	[jot]
8 eight	ութ	[ut]
9 nine	ինը	['inɛ]
10 ten	տաս	[tas]

11 eleven	տասնմեկ	[tasn'mek]
12 twelve	տասներկու	[tasner'ku]
13 thirteen	տասներեք	[tasne'rek]
14 fourteen	տասնչորս	[tasn'tʃors]
15 fifteen	տասնհինգ	[tas'niŋ]

| 16 sixteen | տասնվեց | [tasn'vets] |
| 17 seventeen | տասնյոթ | [tasn'jot] |

18 eighteen	տասնութ	[tas'nut]
19 nineteen	տասնինը	[tas'ninɛ]
20 twenty	քսան	[ksan]
30 thirty	երեսուն	[ere'sun]
40 forty	քառասուն	[kara'sun]
50 fifty	հիսուն	[i'sun]
60 sixty	վաթսուն	[va'tsun]
70 seventy	յոթանասուն	[jotana'sun]
80 eighty	ութսուն	[u'tsun]
90 ninety	իննսուն	[iŋ'sun]
100 one hundred	հարյուր	[ar'jur]
200 two hundred	երկու հարյուր	[er'ku ar'jur]
300 three hundred	երեք հարյուր	[e'rek ar'jur]
400 four hundred	չորս հարյուր	['tʃors ar'jur]
500 five hundred	հինգ հարյուր	['hiŋ ar'jur]
600 six hundred	վեց հարյուր	['vets ar'jur]
700 seven hundred	յոթ հարյուր	['jot ar'jur]
800 eight hundred	ութ հարյուր	['ut ar'jur]
900 nine hundred	ինը հարյուր	['inɛ ar'jur]
1000 one thousand	հազար	[a'zar]
10000 ten thousand	տաս հազար	['tas a'zar]
one hundred thousand	հարյուր հազար	[ar'jur a'zar]
million	միլիոն	[mili'on]
billion	միլիարդ	[mili'ard]

3. Humans. Family

man (adult male)	տղամարդ	[tha'mard]
young man	պատանի	[pata'ni]
teenager	դեռահաս	[dera'as]
woman	կին	[kin]
girl (young woman)	օրիորդ	[ori'ord]
age	տարիք	[ta'rik]
adult (adj)	մեծահասակ	[metsa:'sak]
middle-aged (adj)	միջին տարիքի	[mi'dʒin tari'ki]
elderly (adj)	տարեց	[ta'rets]
old (adj)	ծեր	[tser]
old man	ծերունի	[tseru'ni]
old woman	պառավ	[pa'rav]
retirement	թոշակ	[to'ʃak]
to retire (from job)	թոշակի գնալ	[toʃʌ'ki g'nal]
retiree	թոշակառու	[toʃʌka'ru]

mother	մայր	[majr]
father	հայր	[ajr]
son	որդի	[vor'di]
daughter	դուստր	[dustr]
brother	եղբայր	[eh'bajr]
sister	քույր	[kujr]

parents	ծնողներ	[tsnoh'ner]
child	երեխա	[ere'ha]
children	երեխաներ	[ereha'ner]
stepmother	խորթ մայր	[hort 'majr]
stepfather	խորթ հայր	[hort 'ajr]

grandmother	տատիկ	[ta'tik]
grandfather	պապիկ	[pa'pik]
grandson	թոռ	[tor]
granddaughter	թոռնուհի	[tornu'i]
grandchildren	թոռներ	[tor'ner]

nephew	քրոջորդի, քրոջ աղջիկ	[krodʒor'di], [k'rodʒ ah'dʒik]
niece	եղբորորդի, եղբոր աղջիկ	[ehboror'di, eh'bor ah'dʒik]
wife	կին	[kin]
husband	ամուսին	[amu'sin]
married (masc.)	ամուսնացած	[amusna'tsats]
married (fem.)	ամուսնացած	[amusna'tsats]
widow	այրի կին	[aj'ri 'kin]
widower	այրի տղամարդ	[aj'ri tha'mard]

name (first name)	անուն	[a'nun]
surname (last name)	ազգանուն	[azga'nun]

relative	ազգական	[azga'kan]
friend (masc.)	ընկեր	[i'ŋker]
friendship	ընկերություն	[iŋkeru'tsyn]

partner	գործընկեր	[gortsi'ŋker]
superior (n)	պետ	[pet]
colleague	գործընկեր	[gortsi'ŋker]
neighbors	հարևաններ	[areva'ŋer]

4. Human body

organism (body)	օրգանիզմ	[orga'nizm]
body	մարմին	[mar'min]
heart	սիրտ	[sirt]
blood	արյուն	[a'ryn]
brain	ուղեղ	[u'heh]
nerve	ներվ	[nerv]
bone	ոսկոր	[vos'kor]

skeleton	կմախք	[kmɑhk]
spine (backbone)	ողնաշար	[vohnɑ'ʃʌr]
rib	կողոսկր	[ko'hoskr]
skull	գանգ	[gɑŋ]

muscle	մկան	[mkɑn]
lungs	թոքեր	[to'ker]
skin	մաշկ	[mɑʃk]

head	գլուխ	[gluh]
face	երես	[e'res]
nose	քիթ	[kit]
forehead	ճակատ	[ʧɑ'kɑt]
cheek	այտ	[ɑjt]

mouth	բերան	[be'rɑn]
tongue	լեզու	[le'zu]
tooth	ատամ	[ɑ'tɑm]
lips	շրթունքներ	[ʃrtuŋk'ner]
chin	կզակ	[kzɑk]

ear	ականջ	[ɑ'kɑndʒ]
neck	պարանոց	[pɑrɑ'nots]
throat	կոկորդ	[ko'kord]

eye	աչք	[ɑʧk]
pupil	բիբ	[bib]
eyebrow	ունք	[uŋk]
eyelash	թարթիչ	[tɑr'tiʧ]

hair	մազեր	[mɑ'zer]
hairstyle	սանրվածք	[sɑnr'vɑtsk]
mustache	բեղեր	[be'her]
beard	մորուք	[mo'ruk]
to have (a beard, etc.)	կրել	[krel]
bald (adj)	ճաղատ	[ʧɑ'hɑt]

hand	դաստակ	[dɑs'tɑk]
arm	թև	[tev]
finger	մատ	[mɑt]
nail	եղունգ	[e'huŋ]
palm	ափ	[ɑp]

shoulder	ուս	[us]
leg	ոտք	[votk]
foot	ոտնաթաթ	[votnɑ'tɑt]
knee	ծունկ	[tsuŋk]
heel	կրունկ	[kruŋk]

back	մեջք	[medʒk]
waist	գոտկատեղ	[gotkɑ'teh]
beauty mark	խալ	[hɑl]

5. Medicine. Diseases. Drugs

health	առողջություն	[arohdʒu'tsyn]
well (not sick)	առողջ	[a'rohdʒ]
sickness	հիվանդություն	[ivandu'tsyn]
to be sick	հիվանդ լինել	[i'vand li'nel]
ill, sick (adj)	հիվանդ	[i'vand]
cold (illness)	մրսածություն	[mrsatsu'tsyn]
to catch a cold	մրսել	[mrsel]
tonsillitis	անգինա	[a'ŋina]
pneumonia	թոքերի բորբոքում	[toke'ri borbo'kum]
flu, influenza	գրիպ	[grip]
runny nose (coryza)	հարբուխ	[ar'buh]
cough	հազ	[az]
to cough (vi)	հազալ	[a'zal]
to sneeze (vi)	փռշտալ	[prʃtal]
stroke	ուղեղի կաթված	[uhe'hi kat'vats]
heart attack	ինֆարկտ	[in'farkt]
allergy	ալերգիա	[aler'gia]
asthma	ասթմա	[ast'ma]
diabetes	շաքարախտ	[ʃʌka'raht]
tumor	ուռուցք	[u'rutsk]
cancer	քաղցկեղ	[kahts'keh]
alcoholism	հարբեցողություն	[arbetsohu'tsyn]
AIDS	ՁԻԱՀ	[dzi'ah]
fever	տենդ	[tend]
seasickness	ծովային հիվանդություն	[tsova'jin ivandu'tsyn]
bruise (hématome)	կապտուկ	[kap'tuk]
bump (lump)	ուռուցք	[u'rutsk]
to limp (vi)	կաղալ	[ka'hal]
dislocation	հոդախախտում	[odahah'tum]
to dislocate (vt)	հոդախախտել	[odahah'tel]
fracture	կոտրվածք	[kotr'vatsk]
burn (injury)	այրվածք	[ajr'vatsk]
injury	վնասվածք	[vnas'vatsk]
pain	ցավ	[tsav]
toothache	ատամնացավ	[atamna'tsav]
to sweat (perspire)	քրտնել	[krtnel]
deaf (adj)	խուլ	[hul]
mute (adj)	համր	[amr]
immunity	իմունիտետ	[imuni'tet]
virus	վարակ	[va'rak]
microbe	մանրէ	[man'rɛ]

| bacterium | բակտերիա | [bak'teria] |
| infection | վարակ | [va'rak] |

hospital	հիվանդանոց	[ivanda'nots]
cure	կազդուրում	[kazdu'rum]
to vaccinate (vt)	պատվաստում անել	[patvas'tum a'nel]
to be in a coma	կոմայի մեջ գտնվել	[koma'ji 'medʒ ɪŋk'nel]
intensive care	վերակենդանացում	[verakendana'tsum]
symptom	նախանշան	[nahan'ʃʌn]
pulse	զարկերակ	[zarke'rak]

6. Feelings. Emotions. Conversation

I, me	ես	[es]
you	դու	[du]
he, she, it	նա	[na]

we	մենք	[meŋk]
you (to a group)	դուք	[duk]
they	նրանք	[nraŋk]

Hello! (fam.)	Բարև	[ba'rev]
Hello! (form.)	Բարև՜ ձեզ	[ba'rev 'dzez]
Good morning!	Բարի լույս	[ba'ri 'lujs]
Good afternoon!	Բարի օր	[ba'ri 'or]
Good evening!	Բարի երեկո՜	[ba'ri jere'ko]

to say hello	բարևել	[bare'vel]
to greet (vt)	ողջունել	[vohdʒu'nel]
How are you?	Ո՞նց են գործերդ	['vonts ɛn gor'tserd]
Bye-Bye! Goodbye!	Ցտեսություն	['tsyn]
Thank you!	Շնորհակալություն	[ʃnorakalu'tsyn]

feelings	զգացմունքներ	[zgatsmuŋk'ner]
to be hungry	ուզենալ ուտել	[uze'nal u'tel]
to be thirsty	ուզենալ խմել	[uze'nal h'mel]
tired (adj)	հոգնած	[og'nats]

to be worried	անհանգստանալ	[anaŋsta'nal]
to be nervous	նյարդայնանալ	[nardajna'nal]
hope	հույս	[ujs]
to hope (vi, vt)	հուսալ	[u'sal]

character	բնավորություն	[bnavoru'tsyn]
modest (adj)	համեստ	[a'mest]
lazy (adj)	ծույլ	[tsujl]
generous (adj)	ձեռնատու	[dzerna'rat]
talented (adj)	տաղանդավոր	[tahanda'vor]
honest (adj)	ազնիվ	[az'niv]
serious (adj)	լուրջ	[lurdʒ]

shy, timid (adj)	երկչոտ	[erk'tʃot]
sincere (adj)	անկեղծ	[a'ŋkehts]
coward	վախկոտ	[vah'kot]

to sleep (vi)	քնել	[knel]
dream	երազ	[e'raz]
bed	մահճակալ	[mahtʃa'kal]
pillow	բարձ	[bardz]

insomnia	անքնություն	[aŋknu'tsyn]
to go to bed	գնալ քնելու	[g'nal kne'lu]
nightmare	մղձավանջ	[mhdza'vandʒ]
alarm clock	զարթուցիչ	[zartu'tsitʃ]

smile	ժպիտ	[ʒpit]
to smile (vi)	ժպտալ	[ʒptal]
to laugh (vi)	ծիծաղել	[tsitsa'hel]

quarrel	վեճ	[vetʃ]
insult	վիրավորանք	[viravo'raŋk]
resentment	վիրավորանք	[viravo'raŋk]
angry (mad)	բարկացած	[barka'tsats]

7. Clothing. Personal accessories

clothes	հագուստ	[a'gust]
coat (overcoat)	վերարկու	[verar'ku]
fur coat	մուշտակ	[muʃ'tak]
jacket (e.g., leather ~)	բաճկոն	[batʃ'kon]
raincoat (trenchcoat, etc.)	թիկնոց	[tik'nots]

shirt (button shirt)	վերնաշապիկ	[vernaʃʌ'pik]
pants	տաբատ	[ta'bat]
suit jacket	պիջակ	[pi'dʒak]
suit	կոստյում	[kos'tym]

dress (frock)	զգեստ	[zgest]
skirt	շրջազգեստ	[ʃrdʒaz'gest]
T-shirt	մարզաշապիկ	[marzaʃʌ'pik]
bathrobe	խալաթ	[ha'lat]
pajamas	նվջազգեստ	[ŋdʒaz'gest]
workwear	աշխատանքային համազգեստ	[aʃhataŋka'jın amaz'gest]

underwear	ներքնազգեստ	[nerknaz'gest]
socks	կիսագուլպա	[kisagul'pa]
bra	կրծքակալ	[krtskal]
pantyhose	զուգագուլպա	[zugagul'pa]
stockings (thigh highs)	գուլպաներ	[gulpa'ner]
bathing suit	լողազգեստ	[lohaz'gest]

hat	գլխարկ	[glhark]
footwear	կոշիկ	[ko'ʃik]
boots (cowboy ~)	երկարաճիտ կոշիկներ	[erkara'tʃit koʃik'ner]
heel	կրունկ	[kruŋk]
shoestring	կոշկակապ	[koʃka'kap]
shoe polish	կոշիկի քսուք	[koʃi'ki k'suk]

cotton (n)	բամբակ	[bam'bak]
wool (n)	բուրդ	[burd]
fur (n)	մորթի	[mor'ti]

gloves	ձեռնոցներ	[dzernots'ner]
mittens	ձեռնոց	[dzer'nots]
scarf (muffler)	շարֆ	[ʃʌrf]
glasses (eyeglasses)	ակնոց	[ak'nots]
umbrella	հովանոց	[ova'nots]

tie (necktie)	փողկապ	[poh'kap]
handkerchief	թաշկինակ	[taʃki'nak]
comb	սանր	[sanr]
hairbrush	մազերի խոզանակ	[maze'ri hoza'nak]

buckle	ճարմանդ	[tʃar'mand]
belt	գոտի	[go'ti]
purse	կանացի պայուսակ	[kana'tsi paju'sak]

collar	օձիք	[o'dzik]
pocket	գրպան	[grpan]
sleeve	թեվք	[tevk]
fly (on trousers)	լայնույթ	[laj'nujt]

zipper (fastener)	կայծակաճարմանդ	[kajsaka tʃar'mand]
button	կոճակ	[ko'tʃak]
to get dirty (vi)	կեղտոտվել	[kehtot'vel]
stain (mark, spot)	բիծ	[bits]

8. City. Urban institutions

store	խանութ	[ha'nut]
shopping mall	առևտրի կենտրոն	[arevt'ri kent'ron]
supermarket	սուպերմարքեթ	[supermar'ket]
shoe store	կոշիկի սրահ	[koʃi'ki s'rah]
bookstore	գրախանութ	[graha'nut]

drugstore, pharmacy	դեղատուն	[deha'tun]
bakery	հացաբուլկեղենի խանութ	[atsabulkehe'ni ha'nut]
candy store	հրուշակեղենի խանութ	[ɛruʃʌkehe'ni ha'nut]
grocery store	նպարեղենի խանութ	[nparehe'ni ha'nut]
butcher shop	մսի խանութ	[m'si ha'nut]
produce store	բանջարեղենի կրպակ	[bandʒarehe'ni kr'pak]

market	շուկա	[ʃuˈka]
hair salon	վարսավիրանոց	[varsaviraˈnots]
post office	փոստ	[post]
dry cleaners	քիմմաքրման կետ	[kimmakrˈman ˈket]
circus	կրկես	[krkes]
zoo	կենդանաբանական այգի	[kendanabanaˈkan ajˈgi]

theater	թատրոն	[tatˈron]
movie theater	կինոթատրոն	[kinotatˈron]
museum	թանգարան	[taŋaˈran]
library	գրադարան	[gradaˈran]

mosque	մզկիթ	[mzkit]
synagogue	սինագոգ	[sinaˈgog]
cathedral	տաճար	[taˈtʃar]

| temple | տաճար | [taˈtʃar] |
| church | եկեղեցի | [ekeheˈtsi] |

college	ինստիտուտ	[instiˈtut]
university	համալսարան	[amalsaˈran]
school	դպրոց	[dprots]

| hotel | հյուրանոց | [juraˈnots] |
| bank | բանկ | [baŋk] |

| embassy | դեսպանատուն | [despanaˈtun] |
| travel agency | տուրիստական գործակալություն | [turistaˈkan gortsakaluˈtsyn] |

| subway | մետրո | [metˈro] |
| hospital | հիվանդանոց | [ivandaˈnots] |

| gas station | բենզալցակայան | [benzaltsakaˈjan] |
| parking lot | ավտոկայան | [avtokaˈjan] |

ENTRANCE	ՄՈՒՏՔ	[mutk]
EXIT	ԵԼՔ	[elk]
PUSH	ԴԵՊԻ ԴՈՒՐՍ	[deˈpi ˈdurs]
PULL	ԴԵՊԻ ՆԵՐՍ	[ˈdepi ˈners]

| OPEN | ԲԱՑ Է | [bats ɛ] |
| CLOSED | ՓԱԿ Է | [pak ɛ] |

monument	արձան	[arˈdzan]
fortress	ամրոց	[amˈrots]
palace	պալատ	[paˈlat]

medieval (adj)	միջնադարյան	[midʒnadaˈrian]
ancient (adj)	հինավուրց	[inaˈvurts]
national (adj)	ազգային	[azgaˈjın]
well-known (adj)	հայտնի	[ajtˈni]

9. Money. Finances

money	դրամ	[dram]
coin	մետաղադրամ	[metahad'ram]
dollar	դոլլար	[dol'lar]
euro	եվրո	['evro]

ATM	բանկոմատ	[baŋko'mat]
currency exchange	փոխանակման կետ	[pohanak'man 'ket]
exchange rate	փոխարժեք	[pohar'ʒek]
cash	կանխիկ դրամ	[kan'hik d'ram]

How much?	Որքա՞ն արժե:	[vor'kan ar'ʒe]
to pay (vi, vt)	վճարել	[vtʃa'rel]
payment	վճար	[v'tʃar]
change (give the ~)	մանր	[manr]

price	գին	[gin]
discount	զեղչ	[zehtʃ]
cheap (adj)	էժան	[ɛ'ʒan]
expensive (adj)	թանկ	[taŋk]

bank	բանկ	[baŋk]
account	հաշիվ	[a'ʃiv]
credit card	վարկային քարտ	[varka'jin 'kart]
check	չեք	[tʃek]
to write a check	չեք դուրս գրել	[tʃek durs g'rel]
checkbook	չեքային գրքույկ	[tʃeka'jin gr'kujk]

debt	պարտք	[partk]
debtor	պարտապան	[parta'pan]
to lend (money)	պարտքով տալ	[part'kov 'tal]
to borrow (vi, vt)	պարտքով վերցնել	[part'kov verts'nel]

to rent (~ a tuxedo)	վարձել	[var'dzel]
on credit (adv)	վարկով	[var'kov]
wallet	թղթապանակ	[thtapa'nak]
safe	չհրկիզվող պահարան	[tʃrkiz'voh pa:'ran]
inheritance	ժառանգություն	[ʒaraŋu'tsyn]
fortune (wealth)	ունեցվածք	[unets'vatsk]

tax	հարկ	[ark]
fine	տուգանք	[tu'gaŋk]
to fine (vt)	տուգանել	[tuga'nel]

wholesale (adj)	մեծածախ	[metsa'tsah]
retail (adj)	մանրածախ	[manra'tsah]
to insure (vt)	ապահովագրել	[apaovag'rel]
insurance	ապահովագրություն	[apaovagru'tsyn]
capital	կապիտալ	[kapi'tal]
turnover	շրջանառություն	[ʃrdʒanaru'tsyn]

stock (share)	բաժնետոմս	[baʒne'toms]
profit	շահույթ	[ʃʌ'ujt]
profitable (adj)	շահավետ	[ʃʌɑ'vet]
crisis	ճգնաժամ	[tʃgnɑ'ʒɑm]
bankruptcy	սնանկություն	[snɑŋku'tsyn]
to go bankrupt	սննկանալ	[snɪŋkɑ'nɑl]
accountant	հաշվապահ	[aʃvɑ'pɑh]
salary	աշխատավարձ	[aʃhɑtɑ'vɑrdz]
bonus (money)	պարգեվավճար	[pɑrgevɑv'tʃɑr]

10. Transportation

bus	ավտոբուս	[ɑvto'bus]
streetcar	տրամվայ	[trɑm'vɑj]
trolley bus	տրոլեյբուս	[trolej'bus]
to go by ...	... ով գնալ	[ov g'nɑl]
to get on (~ the bus)	նստել	[nstel]
to get off ...	իջնել	[idʒ'nel]
stop (e.g., bus ~)	կանգառ	[kɑ'ŋɑr]
terminus	վերջին կանգառ	[ver'dʒin kɑ'ŋɑr]
schedule	ժամանակացույց	[ʒɑmɑnɑkɑ'tsujts]
ticket	տոմս	[toms]
to be late (for ...)	ուշանալ	[uʃʌ'nɑl]
taxi, cab	տաքսի	[tɑk'si]
by taxi	տաքսիով	[tɑksi'ov]
taxi stand	տաքսիների կայան	[tɑksine'ri kɑ'jɑn]
traffic	ճանապարհային երթեկնություն	[tʃɑnɑpɑrɑ'jɪn erteveku'tsyn]
rush hour	պիկ ժամ	['pik 'ʒɑm]
to park (vi)	կանգնեցնել	[kɑŋets'nel]
subway	մետրո	[met'ro]
station	կայարան	[kɑjɑ'rɑn]
train	գնացք	[gnɑtsk]
train station	կայարան	[kɑjɑ'rɑn]
rails	գծեր	[gtser]
compartment	կուպե	[ku'pe]
berth	մահճակ	[mɑh'tʃɑk]
airplane	ինքնաթիռ	[iŋknɑ'tir]
air ticket	ավիատոմս	[ɑviɑ'toms]
airline	ավիաընկերություն	[ɑviɑɪŋkeru'tsyn]
airport	օդանավակայան	[odɑnɑvɑkɑ'jɑn]
flight (act of flying)	թռիչք	[tritʃk]

| luggage | ուղեբեռ | [uhe'ber] |
| luggage cart | սայլակ | [saj'lak] |

ship	նավ	[nav]
cruise ship	լայներ	['lajner]
yacht	զբոսանավ	[zbosa'nav]
boat (flat-bottomed ~)	նավակ	[na'vak]

captain	նավապետ	[nava'pet]
cabin	նավասենյակ	[navase'ŋak]
port (harbor)	նավահանգիստ	[nava:'ŋist]

bicycle	հեծանիվ	[ɛtsa'niv]
scooter	մոտոռոլեր	[moto'roller]
motorcycle, bike	մոտոցիկլ	[moto'tsikl]
pedal	ոտնակ	[vot'nak]
pump	պոմպ	[pomp]
wheel	անիվ	[a'niv]

automobile, car	ավտոմեքենա	[avtomeke'na]
ambulance	շտապ օգնություն	[ʃ'tap ognu'tsyn]
truck	բեռնատար	[berna'tar]
used (adj)	օգտագործված	[ogtagorts'vats]
car crash	վթար	[vtar]
repair	նորոգում	[noro'gum]

11. Food. Part 1

meat	միս	[mis]
chicken	հավ	[av]
duck	բադ	[bad]

pork	խոզի միս	[ho'zi 'mis]
veal	հորթի միս	[or'ti 'mis]
lamb	ոչխարի միս	[votʃha'ri 'mis]
beef	տավարի միս	[tava'ri 'mis]

sausage (bologna, pepperoni, etc.)	երշիկ	[er'ʃik]
egg	ձու	[dzu]
fish	ձուկ	[dzuk]
cheese	պանիր	[pa'nir]
sugar	շաքար	[ʃʌ'kar]
salt	աղ	[ah]

rice	բրինձ	[brindz]
pasta	մակարոն	[maka'ron]
butter	երուցքային կարագ	[serutska'jın ka'rag]
vegetable oil	բուսական յուղ	[busa'kan 'juh]
bread	հաց	[hats]

chocolate (n)	շոկոլադ	[ʃoko'lad]
wine	գինի	[gi'ni]
coffee	սուրճ	[surtʃ]
milk	կաթ	[kat]
juice	հյութ	[hjut]
beer	գարեջուր	[gare'dʒur]
tea	թեյ	[tej]

tomato	լոլիկ	[lo'lik]
cucumber	վարունգ	[va'ruŋ]
carrot	գազար	[ga'zar]
potato	կարտոֆիլ	[karto'fil]
onion	սոխ	[soh]
garlic	սխտոր	[shtor]

cabbage	կաղամբ	[ka'hamb]
beetroot	բազուկ	[ba'zuk]
eggplant	սմբուկ	[smbuk]
dill	սամիթ	[sa'mit]
lettuce	սալաթ	[sa'lat]
corn (maize)	եգիպտացորեն	[egiptatso'ren]

fruit	միրգ	[mirg]
apple	խնձոր	[hndzor]
pear	տանձ	[tandz]
lemon	կիտրոն	[kit'ron]
orange	նարինջ	[na'rindʒ]
strawberry	ելակ	[e'lak]

plum	սալոր	[sa'lor]
raspberry	մորի	[mo'ri]
pineapple	արքայախնձոր	[arkajahn'dzor]
banana	բանան	[ba'nan]
watermelon	ձմերուկ	[dzme'ruk]
grape	խաղող	[ha'hoh]
melon	սեխ	[seh]

12. Food. Part 2

cuisine	խոհանոց	[hoa'nots]
recipe	բաղադրատոմս	[bahadra'toms]
food	կերակուր	[kera'kur]

to have breakfast	նախաճաշել	[nahatʃa'ʃel]
to have lunch	ճաշել	[tʃa'ʃel]
to have dinner	ընթրել	[ɪnt'rel]

taste, flavor	համ	[am]
tasty (adj)	համեղ	[a'meh]
cold (adj)	սառը	['sarɪ]

hot (adj)	տաք	[tak]
sweet (sugary)	քաղցր	[kahtsr]
salty (adj)	աղի	[a'hi]

sandwich (bread)	բրդուճ	[brdutʃ]
side dish	գառնիր	[gar'nir]
filling (for cake, pie)	լցոն	[ltson]
sauce	սոուս	[so'us]
piece (of cake, pie)	կտոր	[ktor]

diet	սննդակարգ	[snda'karg]
vitamin	վիտամին	[vita'min]
calorie	կալորիա	[ka'lorija]
vegetarian (n)	բուսակեր	[busa'ker]

restaurant	ռեստորան	[resto'ran]
coffee house	սրճարան	[srtʃa'ran]
appetite	ախորժակ	[ahor'ʒak]
Enjoy your meal!	Բարի՛ ախորժակ:	[ba'ri ahor'ʒak]

waiter	մատուցող	[matu'tsoh]
waitress	մատուցողուհի	[matutsohu'i]
bartender	բարմեն	[bar'men]
menu	մենյու	[me'ny]

| spoon | գդալ | [gdal] |
| knife | դանակ | [da'nak] |

| fork | պատառաքաղ | [patara'kah] |
| cup (e.g., coffee ~) | բաժակ | [ba'ʒak] |

| plate (dinner ~) | ափսե | [ap'se] |
| saucer | պնակ | [pnak] |

| napkin (on table) | անձեռոցիկ | [andzero'tsik] |
| toothpick | ատամնափորիչ | [atamnapo'ritʃ] |

to order (meal)	պատվիրել	[patvi'rel]
course, dish	ճաշատեսակ	[tʃaʃte'sak]
portion	բաժին	[ba'ʒin]
appetizer	խորտիկ	[hor'tik]

| salad | աղցան | [ah'tsan] |
| soup | ապուր | [a'pur] |

dessert	աղանդեր	[ahan'der]
whole fruit jam	մուրաբա	[mura'ba]
ice-cream	պաղպաղակ	[pahpa'hak]

check	հաշիվ	[a'ʃiv]
to pay the check	հաշիվը վճարել	[a'ʃivı pa'kel]
tip	թեյավճար	[teja'poh]

13. House. Apartment. Part 1

house	տուն	[tun]
country house	քաղաքից դուրս տուն	[kaha'kits 'durs 'tun]
villa (seaside ~)	վիլլա	['villa]

floor, story	հարկ	[ark]
entrance	մուտք	[mutk]
wall	պատ	[pat]
roof	տանիք	[ta'nik]
chimney	խողովակ	[hoho'vak]
attic (storage place)	ձեղնահարկ	[dzehna'ark]

window	պատուհան	[patu'an]
window ledge	պատուհանագոգ	[patuana'gog]
balcony	պատշգամբ	[patʃ'gamb]

stairs (stairway)	աստիճան	[asti'tʃan]
mailbox	փոստարկղ	[pos'tarkh]
garbage can	աղբարկղ	[ah'barkh]
elevator	վերելակ	[vere'lak]

electricity	էլեկտրականություն	[ɛlektrakanu'tsyn]
light bulb	լամպ	[lamp]
switch	անջատիչ	[andʒa'titʃ]
wall socket	վարդակ	[var'dak]
fuse	ապահովիչ	[apao'vitʃ]

door	դուռ	[dur]
handle, doorknob	բռնակ	[brnak]
key	բանալի	[bana'li]
doormat	փոքր գորգ	[pokr 'gorg]

door lock	փական	[pa'kan]
doorbell	զանգ	[zaŋ]
knock (at the door)	թակոց	[ta'kots]
to knock (vi)	թակել	[ta'kel]
peephole	դիտանցք	[di'tantsk]

yard	բակ	[bak]
garden	այգի	[aj'gi]
swimming pool	լողավազան	[lohava'zan]
gym (home gym)	սպորտային դահլիճ	[sporta'jın dah'litʃ]
tennis court	թենիսի հարթակ	[teni'si ar'tak]
garage	ավտոտնակ	[avtot'nak]

private property	մասնավոր սեփականություն	[masna'vor sepakanu'tsyn]
warning sign	զգուշացնող գրություն	[zguʃʌts'noh gru'tsyn]
security	պահակություն	[pa:ku'tsyn]
security guard	պահակ	[pa'ak]

renovations	վերանորոգում	[veranoro'gum]
to renovate (vt)	վերանորոգում անել	[veranoro'gum a'nel]
to put in order	կարգի բերել	[kar'gi be'rel]
to paint (~ a wall)	ներկել	[ner'kel]
wallpaper	պաստառ	[pas'tar]
to varnish (vt)	լաքապատել	[lakapa'tel]

pipe	խողովակ	[hoho'vak]
tools	գործիքներ	[gortsik'ner]
basement	նկուղ	[ŋkuh]
sewerage (system)	կոյուղի	[koju'hi]

14. House. Apartment. Part 2

apartment	բնակարան	[bnaka'ran]
room	սենյակ	[se'ɲak]
bedroom	ննջարան	[ŋdʒa'ran]
dining room	ճաշասենյակ	[tʃaʃase'ɲak]

living room	հյուրասենյակ	[jurase'ɲak]
study (home office)	աշխատասենյակ	[aʃhatase'ɲak]
entry room	նախասենյակ	[nahase'ɲak]
bathroom (room with a bath or shower)	լոգարան	[loga'ran]

| half bath | զուգարան | [zuga'ran] |

| floor | հատակ | [a'tak] |
| ceiling | առաստաղ | [aras'tah] |

to dust (vt)	փոշին սրբել	[po'ʃin sr'bel]
vacuum cleaner	փոշեկուլ	[poʃə'kul]
to vacuum (vt)	փոշեկուլով մաքրել	[poʃeku'lov mak'rel]

mop	շվաբր	[ʃvabr]
dust cloth	շնորհ	[dʒŋdʒots]
short broom	ավել	[a'vel]
dustpan	աղբական	[ahba'kal]

furniture	կահույք	[ka'ujk]
table	սեղան	[se'han]
chair	աթոռ	[a'tor]
armchair	բազկաթոռ	[bazka'tor]

bookcase	գրապահարան	[grapa:'ran]
shelf	դարակ	[da'rak]
wardrobe	պահարան	[pa:'ran]

mirror	հայելի	[aje'li]
carpet	գորգ	[gorg]
fireplace	բուխարի	[buha'ri]

drapes	վարագույր	[vara'gujr]
table lamp	սեղանի լամպ	[seha'ni 'lamp]
chandelier	ջահ	[dʒah]

kitchen	խոհանոց	[hoa'nots]
gas stove (range)	գազօջախ	[gazo'dʒah]
electric stove	էլեկտրական սալօջախ	[ɛlektra'kan salo'dʒah]
microwave oven	միկրոալիքային վառարան	[mikroalika'jın vara'ran]

refrigerator	սառնարան	[sarna'ran]
freezer	սառնախցիկ	[sarnah'tsik]
dishwasher	աման լվացող մեքենա	[a'man lva'tsoh meke'na]
faucet	ծորակ	[tso'rak]

meat grinder	մսաղաց	[msa'hats]
juicer	հյութաքամիչ	[jutaka'mitʃ]
toaster	տոստեր	[tos'ter]
mixer	հարիչ	[a'ritʃ]

coffee machine	սրճեփ	[srtʃep]
kettle	թեյնիկ	[tej'nik]
teapot	թեյաման	[teja'man]

TV set	հեռուստացույց	[ɛrusta'tsujts]
VCR (video recorder)	տեսամագնիտոֆոն	[tesamagnito'fon]
iron (e.g., steam ~)	արդուկ	[ar'duk]
telephone	հեռախոս	[ɛra'hos]

15. Professions. Social status

director	տնօրեն	[tno'ren]
superior	պետ	[pet]
president	նախագահ	[naha'ga]
assistant	օգնական	[ogna'kan]
secretary	քարտուղար	[kartu'har]

owner, proprietor	սեփականատեր	[sepakana'ter]
partner	գործընկեր	[gortsı'ŋker]
stockholder	բաժնետեր	[baʒne'ter]

businessman	գործարար	[gortsa'rar]
millionaire	միլիոնատեր	[miliona'ter]
billionaire	միլիարդեր	[miliarda'ter]

actor	դերասան	[dera'san]
architect	ճարտարապետ	[tʃartara'pet]
banker	բանկատեր	[baŋka'ter]
broker	բրոկեր	[b'roker]
veterinarian	անասնաբույժ	[anasna'bujʒ]

doctor	բժիշկ	[bʒiʃk]
chambermaid	սպասավորուհի	[spasavoru'i]
designer	դիզայներ	[dizaj'ner]
correspondent	թղթակից	[thta'kits]
delivery man	առաքիչ	[ara'kitʃ]

electrician	մոնտյոր	[mon'tər]
musician	երաժիշտ	[era'ʒiʃt]
babysitter	դայակ	[da'jak]
hairdresser	վարսահարդար	[varsa:r'dar]
herder, shepherd	հովիվ	[o'viv]

singer (masc.)	երգիչ	[er'gitʃ]
translator	թարգմանիչ	[targma'nitʃ]
writer	գրող	[groh]
carpenter	ատաղձագործ	[atahdza'gorts]
cook	խոհարար	[hoa'rar]

fireman	հրշեջ	[ɛr'ʃedʒ]
police officer	ոստիկան	[vosti'kan]
mailman	փոստատար	[posta'tar]
programmer	ծրագրավորող	[tsragravo'roh]
salesman (store staff)	վաճառող	[vatʃa'roh]

worker	բանվոր	[ban'vor]
gardener	այգեպան	[ajge'pan]
plumber	սանտեխնիկ	[santeh'nik]
dentist	ատամնաբույժ	[atamna'bujʒ]
flight attendant (fem.)	ուղեկցորդուհի	[uhektsordu'i]

dancer (masc.)	պարող	[pa'roh]
bodyguard	թիկնապահ	[tikna'pa]
scientist	գիտնական	[gitna'kan]
schoolteacher	ուսուցիչ	[usu'tsitʃ]

farmer	ֆերմեր	[fer'mer]
surgeon	վիրաբույժ	[vira'bujʒ]
miner	հանքափոր	[anka'por]
chef (kitchen chef)	շեֆ-խոհարար	['ʃef hoa'rar]
driver	վարորդ	[va'rord]

16. Sport

kind of sports	մարզաձև	[marza'dzev]
soccer	ֆուտբոլ	[fut'bol]
hockey	հոկեյ	[ho'kej]
basketball	բասկետբոլ	[basket'bol]
baseball	բեյսբոլ	[bejs'bol]
volleyball	վոլեյբոլ	[volej'bol]
boxing	բռնցքամարտ	[brntska'mart]

wrestling	ըմբշամարտ	[ɪmbʃʌ'mart]
tennis	թենիս	[te'nis]
swimming	լող	[loh]

chess	շախմատ	[ʃʌh'mat]
running	մրցավազք	[mrtsa'vazk]
athletics	թեթև ատլետիկա	[te'tev at'letika]
figure skating	գեղասահք	[geha'sahk]
cycling	հեծանվավազորդ	[ɛtsanvas'port]

billiards	բիլյարդ	[bi'ʎjard]
bodybuilding	բոդիբիլդինգ	[bodi'bildiŋ]
golf	գոլֆ	[goʎf]
scuba diving	դայվինգ	['dajviŋ]
sailing	առագաստանավային սպորտ	[aragastanava'jɪn s'port]
archery	նետաձգություն	[netadzgu'tsyn]

period, half	խաղակես	[haha'kes]
half-time	ընդմիջում	[ɪndmi'dʒum]
tie	ոչ ոքի	['votʃ vo'ki]
to tie (vi)	ոչ ոքի խաղալ	['votʃ vo'ki ha'hal]

treadmill	վազքուղի	[vazku'hi]
player	խաղացող	[haha'tsoh]
substitute	պահեստային խաղացող	[paɛsta'jɪn haha'tsoh]
substitutes bench	պահեստայինների նստարան	[paɛstajɪŋe'ri nsta'ran]

match	հանդիպում	[andi'pum]
goal	դարպաս	[dar'pas]
goalkeeper	դարպասապահ	[darpasa'pa]
goal (score)	գոլ	[gol]

Olympic Games	օլիմպիական խաղեր	[olimpia'kan ha'her]
to set a record	սահմանել ռեկորդ	[sahma'nel re'kord]
final	ավարտ	[a'vart]
champion	չեմպյոն	[tʃempi'on]
championship	առաջնություն	[aradʒnu'tsyn]

winner	հաղթող	[ah'toh]
victory	հաղթանակ	[ahta'nak]
to win (vi)	հաղթել	[ah'tel]
to lose (not win)	պարտվել	[part'vel]
medal	մեդալ	[me'dal]

first place	առաջին տեղ	[ara'dʒin 'teh]
second place	երկրորդ տեղ	[erk'rord 'teh]
third place	երրորդ տեղ	[er'rord 'teh]

| stadium | մարզադաշտ | [marza'daʃt] |
| fan, supporter | մարզասեր | [marza'ser] |

| trainer, coach | մարզիչ | [mar'zitʃ] |
| training | մարզում | [mar'zum] |

17. Foreign languages. Orthography

language	լեզու	[le'zu]
to study (vt)	ուսումնասիրել	[usumnasi'rel]
pronunciation	արտասանություն	[artasanu'tsyn]
accent	ակցենտ	[ak'tsent]

noun	գոյական	[goja'kan]
adjective	ածական	[atsa'kan]
verb	բայ	[baj]
adverb	մակբայ	[mak'baj]

pronoun	դերանուն	[dera'nun]
interjection	ձայնարկություն	[dzajnarku'tsyn]
preposition	նախդիր	[nah'dir]

root	արմատ	[ar'mat]
ending	վերջավորություն	[verdʒavoru'tsyn]
prefix	նախածանց	[naha'tsants]
syllable	վանկ	[vaŋk]
suffix	վերջածանց	[verdʒa'tsants]

stress mark	շեշտ	[ʃeʃt]
period, dot	վերջակետ	[verdʒa'ket]
comma	ստորակետ	[stora'ket]
colon	բութ	[but]
ellipsis	բազմակետ	[bazma'ket]

question	հարց	[arts]
question mark	հարցական նշան	[artsa'kan n'ʃʌn]
exclamation point	բացականչական նշան	[batsakantʃa'kan n'ʃʌn]

in quotation marks	չակերտների մեջ	[tʃakertne'ri 'medʒ]
in parenthesis	փակագծերի մեջ	[pakagtse'ri 'medʒ]
letter	տառ	[tar]
capital letter	մեծատառ	[metsa'tar]

sentence	նախադասություն	[nahadasu'tsyn]
group of words	բառակապակցություն	[barakapaktsu'tsyn]
expression	արտահայտություն	[arta:jtu'tsyn]

subject	ենթակա	[enta'ka]
predicate	ստորոգյալ	[storo'gial]
line	տող	[toh]
paragraph	պարբերություն	[parberu'tsyn]
synonym	հոմանիշ	[oma'niʃ]
antonym	հականիշ	[aka'niʃ]

| exception | բացառություն | [batsaru'tsyn] |
| to underline (vt) | ընդգծել | [ındg'tsel] |

rules	կանոն	[ka'non]
grammar	քերականություն	[kerakanu'tsyn]
vocabulary	բառագիտություն	[baragitu'tsyn]
phonetics	հնչյունաբանություն	[ɛntʃunabanu'tsyn]
alphabet	այբուբեն	[ajbu'ben]

textbook	դասագիրք	[dasa'girk]
dictionary	բառարան	[bara'ran]
phrasebook	զրուցարան	[zrutsa'ran]

word	բառ	[bar]
meaning	իմաստ	[i'mast]
memory	հիշողություն	[iʃohu'tsyn]

18. The Earth. Geography

the Earth	Երկիր	[er'kir]
the globe (the Earth)	երկրագունդ	[erkra'gund]
planet	մոլորակ	[molo'rak]

geography	աշխարհագրություն	[aʃharagru'tsyn]
nature	բնություն	[bnu'tsyn]
map	քարտեզ	[kar'tez]
atlas	ատլաս	[at'las]

in the north	հյուսիսում	[jusi'sum]
in the south	հարավում	[ara'vum]
in the west	արևմուտքում	[arevmut'kum]
in the east	արևելքում	[arevel'kum]

sea	ծով	[tsov]
ocean	օվկիանոս	[ovkia'nos]
gulf (bay)	ծոց	[tsots]
straits	նեղուց	[ne'huts]

continent (mainland)	մայրցամաք	[majrtsa'mak]
island	կղզի	[khzi]
peninsula	թերակղզի	[terakh'zi]
archipelago	արշիպելագ	[arʃipe'lag]

harbor	նավահանգիստ	[nava:'ŋist]
coral reef	մարջանախութ	[mardʒana'hut]
shore	ափ	[ap]
coast	ծովափ	[tso'vap]

| flow (flood tide) | մակընթացություն | [makıntatsu'tsyn] |
| ebb (ebb tide) | տեղատվություն | [tehatvu'tsyn] |

latitude	լայնություն	[lajnu'tsyn]
longitude	երկարություն	[erkaru'tsyn]
parallel	զուգահեռական	[zugaɛra'kan]
equator	հասարակած	[asara'kats]

sky	երկինք	[er'kiŋk]
horizon	հորիզոն	[ori'zon]
atmosphere	մթնոլորտ	[mtno'lort]

mountain	լեռ	[ler]
summit, top	գագաթ	[ga'gat]
cliff	ժայռ	[ʒajr]
hill	բլուր	[blur]

volcano	հրաբուխ	[ɛra'buh]
glacier	սառցադաշտ	[sartsa'daʃt]
waterfall	ջրվեժ	[dʒrveʒ]
plain	հարթավայր	[arta'vajr]

river	գետ	[get]
spring (natural source)	աղբյուր	[ah'byr]
bank (of river)	ափ	[ap]
downstream (adv)	հոսանքն ի վայր	[o'saŋkn 'i 'vajr]
upstream (adv)	հոսանքն ի վեր	[o'saŋkn 'i 'ver]

lake	լիճ	[liʧ]
dam	ամբարտակ	[ambar'tak]
canal	ջրանցք	[dʒ'rantsk]
swamp (marshland)	ճահիճ	[ʧa'iʧ]
ice	սառույց	[sa'rujts]

19. Countries of the world. Part 1

Europe	Եվրոպա	[ev'ropa]
European Union	Եվրոմիություն	[evromiu'tsyn]
European (n)	եվրոպացի	[evropa'tsi]
European (adj)	եվրոպական	[evropa'kan]

Austria	Ավստրիա	[avstria]
Great Britain	Մեծ Բրիտանիա	['mets bri'tania]
England	Անգլիա	['aŋlia]
Belgium	Բելգիա	['beʎgia]
Germany	Գերմանիա	[ger'mania]

Netherlands	Նիդերլանդներ	[niderland'ner]
Holland	Հոլանդիա	[o'landia]
Greece	Հունաստան	[unas'tan]
Denmark	Դանիա	['dania]
Ireland	Իռլանդիա	[ir'landia]
Iceland	Իսլանդիա	[is'landia]

Spain	Իսպանիա	[is'pania]
Italy	Իտալիա	[i'talia]
Cyprus	Կիպրոս	[kip'ros]
Malta	Մալթա	['maʎta]
Norway	Նորվեգիա	[nor'vegia]
Portugal	Պորտուգալիա	[portu'galia]
Finland	Ֆինլանդիա	[fin'landia]
France	Ֆրանսիա	[f'ransia]
Sweden	Շվեդիա	[ʃ'vedia]
Switzerland	Շվեյցարիա	[ʃvej'tsaria]
Scotland	Շոտլանդիա	[ʃot'landia]
Vatican	Վատիկան	[vati'kan]
Liechtenstein	Լիխտենշտայն	[lihtenʃ'tajn]
Luxembourg	Լյուքսեմբուրգ	[lyksem'burg]
Monaco	Մոնակո	[mo'nako]
Albania	Ալբանիա	[al'bania]
Bulgaria	Բուլղարիա	[bul'haria]
Hungary	Վենգրիա	['venria]
Latvia	Լատվիա	['latvia]
Lithuania	Լիտվա	[lit'va]
Poland	Լեհաստան	[leas'tan]
Romania	Ռումինիա	[ru'minia]
Serbia	Սերբիա	['serbia]
Slovakia	Սլովակիա	[slo'vakia]
Croatia	Խորվատիա	[hor'vatia]
Czech Republic	Չեխիա	['tʃehia]
Estonia	Էստոնիա	[ɛs'tonia]
Bosnia and Herzegovina	Բոսնիա և Հերցեգովինա	['bosnia 'ev ɛrtsego'vina]
Macedonia (Republic of ~)	Մակեդոնիա	[make'donia]
Slovenia	Սլովենիա	[slo'venia]
Montenegro	Չեռնոգորիա	[tʃerno'goria]
Belarus	Բելառուս	[bela'rus]
Moldova, Moldavia	Մոլդովա	[mol'dova]
Russia	Ռուսաստան	[rusas'tan]
Ukraine	Ուկրաինա	[ukra'ina]

20. Countries of the world. Part 2

Asia	Ասիա	['asia]
Vietnam	Վիետնամ	[vjet'nam]
India	Հնդկաստան	[ındkas'tan]
Israel	Իսրայել	[isra'jel]
China	Չինաստան	[tʃinas'tan]
Lebanon	Լիբանան	[liba'nan]

Mongolia	Մոնղոլիա	[mon'holia]
Malaysia	Մալայզիա	[ma'lajzia]
Pakistan	Պակիստան	[pakis'tan]
Saudi Arabia	Սաուդյան Արաբիա	[sau'dian a'rabia]

Thailand	Թաիլանդ	[tai'land]
Taiwan	Թայվան	[taj'van]
Turkey	Թուրքիա	['turkia]
Japan	Ճապոնիա	[tʃa'ponia]
Afghanistan	Աֆղանստան	[afhans'tan]

Bangladesh	Բանգլադեշ	[baŋla'deʃ]
Indonesia	Ինդոնեզի	[indo'nezia]
Jordan	Հորդանան	[orda'nan]
Iraq	Իրաք	[i'rak]
Iran	Պարսկաստան	[parskas'tan]

Cambodia	Կամպուչիա	[kampu'tʃia]
Kuwait	Քուվեյթ	[ku'vejt]
Laos	Լաոս	[la'os]
Myanmar	Մյանմար	[mjan'mar]
Nepal	Նեպալ	[ne'pal]

United Arab Emirates	Միավորված Արաբական Էմիրություններ	[miavor'vats araba'kan ɛmirutsy'ŋer]
Syria	Սիրիա	['siria]
Palestine	Պաղեստինյան ինքնավարություն	[pahesti'ŋan iŋknavaru'tsyn]
South Korea	Հարավային Կորեա	[arava'jin ko'rea]
North Korea	Հյուսիսային Կորեա	[jusisa'jin ko'rea]

United States of America	Ամերիկայի Միացյալ Նահանգներ	[amerika'jı mia'tsial na:'ŋer]
Canada	Կանադա	[ka'nada]
Mexico	Մեքսիկա	['meksika]
Argentina	Արգենտինա	[argen'tina]
Brazil	Բրազիլիա	[bra'zilia]

Colombia	Կոլումբիա	[ko'lumbia]
Cuba	Կուբա	['kuba]
Chile	Չիլի	['tʃili]
Venezuela	Վենեսուելա	[venesu'ɛla]
Ecuador	Էկվադոր	[ɛkva'dor]

The Bahamas	Բահամյան կղզիներ	[ba:'mian khzi'ner]
Panama	Պանամա	[pa'nama]
Egypt	Եգիպտոս	[egip'tos]
Morocco	Մարոկկո	[ma'rokko]
Tunisia	Թունիս	[tu'nis]

Kenya	Քենիա	['kenia]
Libya	Լիբիա	['libia]

South Africa	Հարավ-Աֆրիկյան հանրապետություն	[a'rav afri'k'an anrapetu'tsyn]
Australia	Ավստրալիա	[avst'ralia]
New Zealand	Նոր Զելանդիա	['nor ze'landia]

21. Weather. Natural disasters

weather	եղանակ	[eha'nak]
weather forecast	եղանակի տեսություն	[ehana'ki tesu'tsyn]
temperature	ջերմաստիճան	[dʒermasti'tʃan]
thermometer	ջերմաչափ	[dʒerma'tʃap]
barometer	ծանրաչափ	[tsanra'tʃap]

sun	արև	[a'rev]
to shine (vi)	շողալ	[ʃo'hal]
sunny (day)	արևային	[areva'jın]
to come up (vi)	ծագել	[tsa'gel]
to set (vi)	մայր մտնել	['majr mt'nel]

rain	անձրև	[andz'rev]
it's raining	անձրև է գալիս	[andz'rev ɛ ga'lis]
pouring rain	տեղատարափ անձրև	[tehata'rap andz'rev]
rain cloud	թուխպ	[tuhp]
puddle	ջրակույտ	[dʒra'kujt]
to get wet (in rain)	թրջվել	[trdʒvel]

thunderstorm	փոթորիկ	[poto'rik]
lightning (~ strike)	կայծակ	[kaj'tsak]
to flash (vi)	փայլատակել	[pajlata'kel]
thunder	որոտ	[vo'rot]
it's thundering	ամպերը որոտում են	[am'peri voro'tum 'ɛn]
hail	կարկուտ	[kar'kut]
it's hailing	կարկուտ է գալիս	[kar'kut ɛ ga'lis]

heat (extreme ~)	տապ	[tap]
it's hot	շոգ է	['ʃog ɛ]
it's warm	տաք է	['tak ɛ]
it's cold	ցուրտ է	['tsurt ɛ]

fog (mist)	մառախուղ	[mara'huh]
foggy	մառախլապատ	[marahla'pat]
cloud	ամպ	[amp]
cloudy (adj)	ամպամած	[ampa'mats]
humidity	խոնավություն	[honavu'tsyn]

snow	ձյուն	[dzyn]
it's snowing	ձյուն է գալիս	['dzyn ɛ ga'lis]
frost (severe ~, freezing cold)	սառնամանիք	[sarnama'nik]
below zero (adv)	զրոյից ցածր	[zro'jıts 'tsatsr]

hoarfrost	եղյամ	[e'ham]
bad weather	վատ եղանակ	['vat eha'nak]
disaster	աղետ	[a'het]
flood, inundation	հեղեղում	[ehe'hum]
avalanche	հուփն	[u'sin]
earthquake	երկրաշարժ	[erkra'ʃʌrʒ]

tremor, quake	ցնցում	[ʦnʦum]
epicenter	էպիկենտրոն	[ɛpikent'ron]
eruption	ժայթքում	[ʒajt'kum]
lava	լավա	['lava]

tornado	տորնադո	[tor'nado]
twister	մրրկային	[mrrka'syn]
hurricane	մրրիկ	[mrrik]
tsunami	ցունամի	[ʦu'nami]
cyclone	ցիկլոն	[ʦik'lon]

22. Animals. Part 1

| animal | կենդանի | [kenda'ni] |
| predator | գիշատիչ | [giʃʌ'tiʧ] |

tiger	վագր	[vagr]
lion	առյուծ	[a'ryʦ]
wolf	գայլ	[gajl]
fox	աղվես	[ah'ves]
jaguar	հովազ	[o'vaz]

lynx	լուսան	[lu'san]
coyote	կոյոտ	[ko'jot]
jackal	շնագայլ	[ʃna'gajl]
hyena	բորենի	[bore'ni]

squirrel	սկյուռ	[skyr]
hedgehog	ոզնի	[voz'ni]
rabbit	ճագար	[ʧa'gar]
raccoon	ջրարջ	[dʒrardʒ]

hamster	գերմանամուկ	[germana'muk]
mole	խլուրդ	[hlurd]
mouse	մուկ	[muk]
rat	առնետ	[ar'net]
bat	չղջիկ	[ʧhdʒik]

beaver	կուղբ	[kuhb]
horse	ձի	[dzi]
deer	եղջերու	[ehdʒe'ru]
camel	ուղտ	[uht]
zebra	զեբր	[zebr]

whale	կետ	[ket]
seal	փոկ	[pok]
walrus	ծովափիղ	[tsova'pih]
dolphin	դելֆին	[deʌ'fin]

bear	արջ	[ardʒ]
monkey	կապիկ	[ka'pik]
elephant	փիղ	[pih]
rhinoceros	ռնգեղջյուր	[rŋeh'dʒyr]
giraffe	ընձուղտ	[ɪn'dzuht]

hippopotamus	գետաձի	[geta'dzi]
kangaroo	ագևազ	[age'vaz]
cat	կատու	[ka'tu]
dog	շուն	[ʃun]

cow	կով	[kov]
bull	ցուլ	[tsul]
sheep (ewe)	ոչխար	[votʃ'har]
goat	այծ	[ajts]

donkey	ավանակ	[ava'nak]
pig, hog	խոզ	[hoz]
hen (chicken)	հավ	[av]
rooster	աքլոր	[ak'lor]

duck	բադ	[bad]
goose	սագ	[sag]
turkey (hen)	հնդկահավ	[ɪndka'av]
sheepdog	հովվաշուն	[ovva'ʃun]

23. Animals. Part 2

bird	թռչուն	[trtʃun]
pigeon	աղավնի	[ahav'ni]
sparrow	ճնճղուկ	[tʃŋtʃhuk]
tit	երաշտահավ	[eraʃta'av]
magpie	կաչաղակ	[katʃa'hak]

eagle	արծիվ	[ar'tsiv]
hawk	շահեն	[ʃʌ'ɛn]
falcon	բազե	[ba'ze]

swan	կարապ	[ka'rap]
crane	կռունկ	[kruŋk]
stork	արագիլ	[ara'gil]
parrot	թութակ	[tu'tak]
peacock	սիրամարգ	[sira'marg]
ostrich	ջայլամ	[dʒaj'lam]
heron	ձկնկուլ	[dzkŋkul]

nightingale	սոխակ	[so'hak]
swallow	ծիծեռնակ	[tsitser'nak]
woodpecker	փայտփորիկ	[pajtpo'rik]
cuckoo	կկու	[kı'ku]
owl	բու	[bu]
penguin	պինգվին	[piŋ'vin]
tuna	թյունոս	[ty'ŋos]
trout	իշխան	[iʃ'han]
eel	օձաձուկ	[odza'dzuk]
shark	շնաձուկ	[ʃna'dzuk]
crab	ծովախեցգետին	[tsovahetsge'tin]
jellyfish	մեդուզա	[me'duza]
octopus	ութոտնուկ	[utvot'nuk]
starfish	ծովաստղ	[tso'vasth]
sea urchin	ծովոզնի	[tsovoz'ni]
seahorse	ծովաձի	[tsova'dzi]
shrimp	մանր ծովախեցգետին	['manr tsovahetsge'tin]
snake	օձ	[odz]
viper	իժ	[iʒ]
lizard	մողես	[mo'hes]
iguana	իգուանա	[igu'ana]
chameleon	քամելեոն	[kamele'on]
scorpion	կարիճ	[ka'ritʃ]
turtle	կրիա	[kri'a]
frog	գորտ	[gort]
crocodile	կոկորդիլոս	[kokordi'los]
insect, bug	միջատ	[mi'dʒat]
butterfly	թիթեռ	[ti'ter]
ant	մրջուն	[mrdʒun]
fly	ճանճ	[tʃantʃ]
mosquito	մծակ	[mo'tsak]
beetle	բզեզ	[bzez]
bee	մեղու	[me'hu]
spider	սարդ	[sard]

24. Trees. Plants

tree	ծառ	[tsar]
birch	կեչի	[ke'tʃi]
oak	կաղնի	[kah'ni]
linden tree	լորի	[lo'ri]
aspen	կաղամախի	[kahama'hi]
maple	թխկի	[thki]

spruce	եղեվնի	[ehev'ni]
pine	սոճի	[so'tʃi]
cedar	մայրի	[maj'ri]
poplar	բարդի	[bar'di]
rowan	սնձենի	[sndze'ni]
beech	հաճարենի	[atʃare'ni]
elm	ծփի	[tspi]
ash (tree)	հացենի	[atse'ni]
chestnut	շագանակենի	[ʃʌganake'ni]
palm tree	արմավենի	[armave'ni]
bush	թուփ	[tup]
mushroom	սունկ	[suŋk]
poisonous mushroom	թունավոր սունկ	[tuna'vor 'suŋk]
cep (Boletus edulis)	սպիտակ սունկ	[spi'tak 'suŋk]
russula	դառնամատիտեղ	[darnamati'teh]
fly agaric	ճանճասպան	[tʃantʃas'pan]
death cap	թունավոր սունկ	[tuna'vor 'suŋk]
flower	ծաղիկ	[tsa'hik]
bouquet (of flowers)	ծաղկեփունջ	[tsahke'pundʒ]
rose (flower)	վարդ	[vard]
tulip	վարդակակաչ	[vardaka'katʃ]
carnation	մեխակ	[me'hak]
camomile	երիցուկ	[eri'tsuk]
cactus	կակտուս	['kaktus]
lily of the valley	հովտաշուշան	[ovtaʃu'ʃʌn]
snowdrop	ձնծաղիկ	[dzntsa'hik]
water lily	շրաշուշան	[dʒraʃu'ʃʌn]
greenhouse (tropical ~)	ջերմոց	[dʒer'mots]
lawn	գազոն	[ga'zon]
flowerbed	ծաղկաթումբ	[tsahka'tumb]
plant	բույս	[bujs]
grass	խոտ	[hot]
leaf	տերև	[te'rev]
petal	թերթիկ	[ter'tik]
stem	ցողուն	[tso'hun]
young plant (shoot)	ծիլ	[tsil]
cereal crops	հացահատիկային բույսեր	[atsa:tika'jın buj'ser]
wheat	ցորեն	[tso'ren]
rye	տարեկան	[tare'kan]
oats	վարսակ	[var'sak]
millet	կորեկ	[ko'rek]
barley	գարի	[ga'ri]
corn	եգիպտացորեն	[egiptatso'ren]
rice	բրինձ	[brindz]

25. Various useful words

balance (of situation)	հավասարակշռություն	[avasarakʃru'tsyn]
base (basis)	հիմք	[imk]
beginning	սկիզբ	[skizb]
category	տեսակ	[te'sak]
choice	ընտրություն	[ıntru'tsyn]
coincidence	համընկնում	[amıŋk'num]
comparison	համեմատություն	[amematu'tsyn]
degree (extent, amount)	աստիճան	[asti'tʃan]
development	զարգացում	[zarga'tsum]
difference	տարբերություն	[tarberu'tsyn]
effect (e.g., of drugs)	արդյունք	[ar'dyŋk]
effort (exertion)	ջանք	[dʒaŋk]
element	տարր	[tarr]
example (illustration)	օրինակ	[ori'nak]
fact	փաստ	[past]
help	օգնություն	[ognu'tsyn]
ideal	իդեալ	[ide'al]
kind (sort, type)	ձև	[dzev]
mistake, error	սխալմունք	[shal'muŋk]
moment	պահ	[pah]
obstacle	խոչընդոտ	[hotʃın'dot]
part (~ of sth)	մաս	[mas]
pause (break)	դադար	[da'dar]
position	դիրք	[dirk]
problem	խնդիր	[hndir]
process	ընթացք	[ın'tatsk]
progress	առաջադիմություն	[aradʒadimu'tsyn]
property (quality)	հատկություն	[atku'tsyn]
reaction	ռեակցիա	[re'aktsia]
risk	ռիսկ	[risk]
secret	գաղտնիք	[gaht'nik]
series	շարք	[ʃʌrk]
shape (outer form)	տեսք	[tesk]
situation	իրադրություն	[iradru'tsyn]
solution	լուծում	[lu'tsum]
standard (adj)	ստանդարտային	[standarta'jın]
stop (pause)	ընդմիջում	[ındmi'dʒum]
style	ոճ	[votʃ]
system	համակարգ	[ama'karg]

table (chart)	աղյուսակ	[ahy'sak]
tempo, rate	տեմպ	[temp]
term (word, expression)	տերմին	[ter'min]
truth (e.g., moment of ~)	ճշմարտություն	[tʃmartu'tsyn]
turn (please wait your ~)	հերթականություն	[ɛrtakanu'tsyn]
urgent (adj)	շտապ	[ʃtap]
utility (usefulness)	օգուտ	[o'gut]
variant (alternative)	տարբերակ	[tarbe'rak]
way (means, method)	միջոց	[mi'dʒots]
zone	հատված	[at'vats]

26. Modifiers. Adjectives. Part 1

additional (adj)	լրացուցիչ	[lratsu'tsitʃ]
ancient (~ civilization)	հնամյա	[ɛna'mʲa]
artificial (adj)	արհեստական	[arɛsta'kan]
bad (adj)	վատ	[vat]
beautiful (person)	գեղեցիկ	[gehe'tsik]
big (in size)	մեծ	[mets]
bitter (taste)	դառը	['darı]
blind (sightless)	կույր	[kujr]
central (adj)	կենտրոնական	[kentrona'kan]
children's (adj)	մանկական	[manka'kan]
clandestine (secret)	ընդհատակյա	[ındata'kʲa]
clean (free from dirt)	մաքուր	[ma'kur]
clever (smart)	խելացի	[hela'tsi]
compatible (adj)	համատեղելի	[amatehe'li]
contented (satisfied)	գոհ	[goh]
dangerous (adj)	վտանգավոր	[vtaŋa'vor]
dead (not alive)	մեռած	[me'rats]
dense (fog, smoke)	թանձր	[tandzr]
difficult (decision)	բարդ	[bard]
dirty (not clean)	կեղտոտ	[keh'tot]
easy (not difficult)	հեշտ	[ɛʃt]
empty (glass, room)	դատարկ	[da'tark]
exact (amount)	ճշգրիտ	[tʃgrit]
excellent (adj)	հիանալի	[iana'li]
excessive (adj)	գեր	[ger]
exterior (adj)	արտաքին	[arta'kin]
fast (quick)	արագ	[a'rag]
fertile (land, soil)	բերրախատ	[berka'rat]
fragile (china, glass)	փխրուն	[phrun]
free (at no cost)	անվճար	[anv'tʃar]

fresh (~ water)	թարմրահամ	[kahtsra'am]
frozen (food)	սառեցված	[sarets'vats]
full (completely filled)	լի	[li]
happy (adj)	երջանիկ	[erdʒa'nik]
hard (not soft)	կոշտ	[koʃt]
huge (adj)	հսկա	[ɛs'ka]
ill (sick, unwell)	հիվանդ	[i'vand]
immobile (adj)	անշարժ	[an'ʃʌrʒ]
important (adj)	կարևոր	[kare'vor]
interior (adj)	ներքին	[ner'kin]
last (e.g., ~ week)	անցյալ	[an'tsʲal]
last (final)	վերջին	[ver'dʒin]
left (e.g., ~ side)	ձախ	[dzah]
legal (legitimate)	օրինական	[orina'kan]
light (in weight)	թեթև	[te'tev]
liquid (fluid)	հրալի	[dʒ'rali]
long (e.g., ~ hair)	երկար	[er'kar]
loud (voice, etc.)	բարձր	[bardzr]
low (voice)	ցածր	[tsatsr]

27. Modifiers. Adjectives. Part 2

main (principal)	գլխավոր	[glha'vor]
matt, matte	փայլատ	[paj'lat]
mysterious (adj)	հանելուկային	[aneluka'jın]
narrow (street, etc.)	նեղ	[neh]
native (~ country)	հայրենի	[ajre'ni]
negative (~ response)	բացասական	[batsasa'kan]
new (adj)	նոր	[nor]
next (e.g., ~ week)	հաջորդ	[a'dʒord]
normal (adj)	նորմալ	[nor'mal]
not difficult (adj)	դյուրին	[dy'rin]
obligatory (adj)	պարտադիր	[parta'dir]
old (house)	ծեր	[tser]
open (adj)	բաց	[bats]
opposite (adj)	հակառակ	[aka'rak]
ordinary (usual)	հասարակ	[asa'rak]
original (unusual)	յուրօրինակ	[jurori'nak]
personal (adj)	անձնական	[andzna'kan]
polite (adj)	հարգալից	[arga'lits]
poor (not rich)	աղքատ	[ah'kat]
possible (adj)	հնարավոր	[ɛnara'vor]
principal (main)	հիմնական	[imna'kan]

probable (adj)	հավանական	[avana'kan]
prolonged (e.g., ~ applause)	տևական	[teva'kan]
public (open to all)	հասարակական	[asaraka'kan]

rare (adj)	հազվագյուտ	[azva'gyt]
raw (uncooked)	հում	[um]
right (not left)	աջ	[adʒ]
ripe (fruit)	հասած	[a'sats]

risky (adj)	ռիսկային	[riska'jın]
sad (~ look)	տխուր	[thur]
second hand (adj)	օգտագործված	[ogtagorts'vats]
shallow (water)	ծանծաղ	[tsan'tsah]
sharp (blade, etc.)	սուր	[sur]

short (in length)	կարճ	[kartʃ]
similar (adj)	նման	[nman]
small (in size)	փոքր	[pokr]
smooth (surface)	հարթ	[art]
soft (~ toys)	փափուկ	[pa'puk]

solid (~ wall)	ամուր	[a'mur]
sour (flavor, taste)	թթու	[ttu]
spacious (house, etc.)	ընդարձակ	[ındar'dzak]
special (adj)	հատուկ	[a'tuk]

straight (line, road)	ուղիղ	[u'hih]
strong (person)	ուժեղ	[u'ʒeh]
stupid (foolish)	հիմար	[i'mar]
superb, perfect (adj)	գերազանց	[gera'zants]

sweet (sugary)	քաղցր	[kahtsr]
tan (adj)	արևառ	[are'var]
tasty (delicious)	համեղ	[a'meh]
unclear (adj)	ոչ պարզ	[votʃ 'parz]

28. Verbs. Part 1

to accuse (vt)	մեղադրել	[mehad'rel]
to agree (say yes)	համաձայնվել	[amadzajn'vel]
to announce (vt)	հայտարարել	[ajtara'rel]
to answer (vi, vt)	պատասխանել	[patasha'nel]
to apologize (vi)	ներողություն խնդրել	[nerohu'tsyn hnd'rel]

to arrive (vi)	ժամանել	[ʒama'nel]
to ask (~ oneself)	հարցնել	[arts'nel]
to be absent	բացակայել	[batsaka'el]
to be afraid	վախենալ	[vahe'nal]
to be born	ծնվել	[tsnvel]

to be in a hurry	շտապել	[ʃta'pel]
to beat (to hit)	հարվածել	[arva'tsel]
to begin (vt)	սկսել	[sksel]
to believe (in God)	հավատալ	[ava'tal]
to belong to …	պատկանել	[patka'nel]
to break (split into pieces)	կոտրել	[kot'rel]
to build (vt)	կառուցել	[karu'tsel]
to buy (purchase)	գնել	[gnel]
can (v aux)	կարողանալ	[karoha'nal]
can (v aux)	կարողանալ	[karoha'nal]
to cancel (call off)	չեղարկել	[tʃehar'kel]
to catch (vt)	բռնել	[brnel]
to change (vt)	փոխել	[po'hel]
to check (to examine)	ստուգել	[stu'gel]
to choose (select)	ընտրել	[ınt'rel]
to clean up (tidy)	մաքրել	[mak'rel]
to close (vt)	փակել	[pa'kel]
to compare (vt)	համեմատել	[amema'tel]
to complain (vi, vt)	գանգատվել	[gaŋat'vel]
to confirm (vt)	հաստատել	[asta'tel]
to congratulate (vt)	շնորհավորել	[ʃnoravo'rel]
to cook (dinner)	պատրաստել	[patras'tel]
to copy (vt)	պատճենել	[patʃe'nel]
to cost (vt)	արժենալ	[arʒe'nal]
to count (add up)	հաշվել	[aʃ'vel]
to count on …	հույս դնել … վրա	[ujs dnel v'ra]
to create (vt)	ստեղծել	[steh'tsel]
to cry (weep)	լացել	[la'tsel]
to dance (vi, vt)	պարել	[pa'rel]
to deceive (vi, vt)	խաբել	[ha'bel]
to decide (~ to do sth)	որոշել	[voro'ʃel]
to delete (vt)	հեռացնել	[ɛrats'nel]
to demand (request firmly)	պահանջել	[pa:n'dʒel]
to deny (vt)	ժխտել	[ʒhtel]
to depend on …	կախված լինել	[kah'vats li'nel]
to despise (vt)	արհամարհել	[arama'rel]
to die (vi)	մահանալ	[ma:'nal]
to dig (vt)	փորել	[po'rel]
to disappear (vi)	անհայտանալ	[anajta'nal]
to discuss (vt)	քննարկել	[kŋar'kel]
to disturb (vt)	անհանգստացնել	[ananŋstats'nel]

29. Verbs. Part 2

to dive (vi)	սուզվել	[suz'vel]
to divorce (vi)	ամուսնալուծվել	[amusnaluts'vel]
to do (vt)	անել	[a'nel]
to doubt (have doubts)	կասկածել	[kaska'tsel]
to drink (vi, vt)	ըմպել	[ɪm'pel]
to drop (let fall)	վայր գցել	['vajr gtsel]
to dry (clothes, hair)	չորացնել	[tʃorats'nel]
to eat (vi, vt)	ուտել	[u'tel]
to end (~ a relationship)	դադարեցնել	[dadarets'nel]
to excuse (forgive)	ներել	[ne'rel]
to exist (vi)	գոյություն ունենալ	[goju'tsyn une'nal]
to expect (foresee)	կանխատեսել	[kanhate'sel]
to explain (vt)	բացատրել	[batsat'rel]
to fall (vi)	ընկնել	[ɛŋk'nel]
to fight (street fight, etc.)	կռվել	[krvel]
to find (vt)	գտնել	[gtnel]
to finish (vt)	ավարտել	[avar'tel]
to fly (vi)	թռչել	[trtʃel]
to forbid (vt)	արգելել	[arge'lel]
to forget (vi, vt)	մոռանալ	[mora'nal]
to forgive (vt)	ներել	[ne'rel]
to get tired	հոգնել	[og'nel]
to give (vt)	տալ	[tal]
to go (on foot)	գնալ	[gnal]
to hate (vt)	ատել	[a'tel]
to have (vt)	ունենալ	[une'nal]
to have breakfast	նախաճաշել	[nahatʃa'ʃel]
to have dinner	ընթրել	[ɪnt'rel]
to have lunch	ճաշել	[tʃa'ʃel]
to hear (vt)	լսել	[lsel]
to help (vt)	օգնել	[og'nel]
to hide (vt)	թաքցնել	[takts'nel]
to hope (vi, vt)	հուսալ	[u'sal]
to hunt (vi, vt)	որս անել	['vors a'nel]
to hurry (vi)	շտապել	[ʃta'pel]
to insist (vi, vt)	պնդել	[pndel]
to insult (vt)	վիրավորել	[viravo'rel]
to invite (vt)	հրավիրել	[ɛravi'rel]
to joke (vi)	կատակել	[kata'kel]
to keep (vt)	պահպանել	[pahpa'nel]
to kill (vt)	սպանել	[spa'nel]
to know (sb)	ճանաչել	[tʃana'tʃel]

to know (sth)	իմանալ	[ima'nal]
to like (I like ...)	դուր գալ	['dur gal]
to look at ...	նայել	[na'el]

to lose (umbrella, etc.)	կորցնել	[korts'nel]
to love (sb)	սիրել	[si'rel]
to make a mistake	սխալվել	[shal'vel]
to meet (vi, vt)	հանդիպել	[andi'pel]
to miss (school, etc.)	բաց թողնել	['bats toh'nel]

30. Verbs. Part 3

to obey (vi, vt)	ենթարկվել	[entark'vel]
to open (vt)	բացել	[ba'tsel]
to participate (vi)	մասնակցել	[masnak'tsel]
to pay (vi, vt)	վճարել	[vtʃa'rel]
to permit (vt)	թույլատրել	[tujlat'rel]

to play (children)	խաղալ	[ha'hal]
to pray (vi, vt)	աղոթել	[aho'tel]
to promise (vt)	խոստանալ	[hosta'nal]
to propose (vt)	առաջարկել	[aradʒar'kel]
to prove (vt)	ապացուցել	[apatsu'tsel]
to read (vi, vt)	կարդալ	[kar'dal]

to receive (vt)	ստանալ	[sta'nal]
to rent (sth from sb)	վարձել	[var'dzel]
to repeat (say again)	կրկնել	[krknel]
to reserve, to book	ամրագրել	[amrag'rel]
to run (vi)	վազել	[va'zel]

to save (rescue)	փրկել	[prkel]
to say (~ thank you)	ասել	[a'sel]
to see (vt)	տեսնել	[tes'nel]
to sell (vt)	վաճառել	[vatʃa'rel]
to send (vt)	ուղարկել	[uhar'kel]
to shoot (vi)	կրակել	[kra'kel]

to shout (vi)	բղավել	[bha'vel]
to show (vt)	ցույց տալ	['tsujts tal]
to sign (document)	ստորագրել	[storag'rel]
to sing (vi)	դայլայլել	[dajlaj'lel]
to sit down (vi)	նստել	[nstel]

to smile (vi)	ժպտալ	[ʒptal]
to speak (vi, vt)	խոսել	[ho'sel]
to steal (money, etc.)	գողանալ	[goha'nal]
to stop (please ~ calling me)	դադարեցնել	[dadarets'nel]
to study (vt)	ուսումնասիրել	[usumnasi'rel]

to swim (vi)	լողալ	[lo'hal]
to take (vt)	վերցնել	[verts'nel]
to talk to …	խոսել … հետ	[ho'sel 'ɛt]
to tell (story, joke)	պատմել	[pat'mel]
to thank (vt)	շնորհակալություն հայտնել	[ʃnorakalu'tsyn ajt'nel]
to think (vi, vt)	մտածել	[mta'tsel]
to translate (vt)	թարգմանել	[targma'nel]
to trust (vt)	վստահել	[vsta'ɛl]
to try (attempt)	փորձել	[por'dzel]
to turn (e.g., ~ left)	թեքվել	[tɛk'vel]
to turn off	անջատել	[andʒa'tel]
to turn on	միացնել	[miats'nel]
to understand (vt)	հասկանալ	[aska'nal]
to wait (vt)	սպասել	[spa'sel]
to want (wish, desire)	ուզենալ	[uze'nal]
to work (vi)	աշխատել	[aʃha'tel]
to write (vt)	գրել	[grel]

33248903R00066

Printed in Great Britain
by Amazon